NEW DESIGNS IN
KINDERGARTENS

DESIGN GUIDE + 31 CASE STUDIES

LINKS

NEW DESIGNS IN KINDERGARTENS

Edition 2014

Author: Jure Kotnik

Work conception: Carles Broto

Editorial coordination: Jacobo Krauel

Graphic design & production: Xavier Broto & Oriol Vallès

Manual design: Andreja Kotnik [Kikographics]

Cover design: Oriol Vallès, graphic designer

Manual design consultant: Domen Fras

Diagrams design: Jure Kotnik, Andreja Kotnik

Text: Contributed by the architects, edited by Emily McBride

© LinksBooks

Jonqueres, 10, 1-5

08003 Barcelona, Spain

Tel.: +34-93-301-21-99

info@linksbooks.net

www.linksbooks.net

NEW DESIGNS IN
KINDERGARTENS

DESIGN GUIDE + 31 CASE STUDIES

LINKS

INDEX

INTRODUCTION

In recent years contemporary day care centers for children have been appearing everywhere, announcing a renaissance in kindergarten architecture. Social change, new regulations and sustainable technologies have meant that the old patterns of kindergarten design have given way to new approaches: innovative, child-centred design and ecological features combined with contemporary design sensibilities. Bland, functional kindergartens are being replaced with bold, colourful architecture in all shapes and sizes, catching the attention of children, parents, architects and the media. Media coverage has further motivated architects to search for innovative solutions and has boosted the popularity of kindergarten projects: there is palpable competition between architects to come up with the most creative design. An assignment for a kindergarten can be a stepping stone for young architects as well as a challenge for established.

Changes in kindergarten architecture have been in part initiated by pedagogical innovations, such as new teaching techniques that focus more on the individual child, and in part by the inclusion of new activities in the curriculum, such as yoga, language courses or computer science. The new approaches promote the child's right to choose, connect facts and communicate. They give children the freedom to think, experience, explore, question and look for answers themselves. Nursery practitioners take on a new role in watching play develop rather than directing it: children are therefore given the freedom to be more creative, which enhances their communication skills. As children are more engaged, this reduces disruptive behaviour, fosters good student-teacher relationships, promotes discovery learning and devolves responsibility for their learning to the children themselves. Kindergartens are becoming a sum of diverse environments rather than a sum of uniform playrooms. Space and materials are carefully arranged to promote active learning, while playrooms are divided into interest areas organized around specific kinds of play, such as for playing with small toys, books, sand-and-water or for playing at houses or doing art activities. Trends show that kindergartens are increasingly adjusting to diverse programmes and becoming more specialized. There are thematic kindergartens that focus on specific activities such as art, healthy living or nature. Sustainable architecture approaches in designing kindergartens supports the use of environmentally-friendly and energy-saving materials in making buildings pleasant for their users and giving them a fun look.

This book is a cross section of the most recent best practice kindergarten projects and presents examples from around the globe. Their situations are diverse but they all show how architects successfully confronted the task of designing day care centres to meet the needs of contemporary children and parents. Some of the selected projects were commissioned by local authorities while others are privately run or run by religious foundations. This shows that the state is gradually giving away some of its control and that today kindergartens are by no means the exclusive domain of local authorities. Furthermore, the selected projects demonstrate that quality kindergartens can be built in any location, including the countryside, on the edge of a wood, in city parks and densely built urban areas.

New Kindergarten Architecture is the most comprehensive selection of contemporary kindergarten projects to date, demonstrating the imaginative solutions used in each situation, tailor-made to the location, programmes and special needs of their small users.

KINDERGARTEN DESIGN MANUAL

Preface:

This manual is intended for architects, to give them an insight into the possibilities in kindergarten design and provide them with practical design guidelines. The manual contains general recommendations, summarized from various national and local building regulations from around the world. A kindergarten must provide safe, interesting and healthy environments to allow children to engage in various stimulating activities important to their development. Good spatial design is therefore very important. In this manual the term "kindergarten" is used to refer to a child care center catering for children in any age group between 0 and 5 years old.

Longest recommended distance from home to kindergarten:

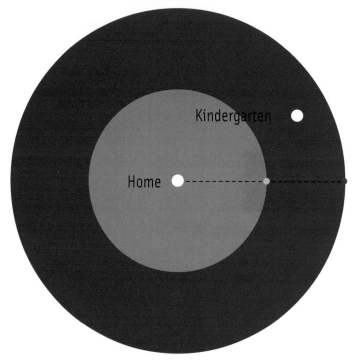

- 500 m
- 1000 m

15min walk for a 3-year old child

The design of a kindergarten should answer the needs of all its users.

A kindergarten usually serves its immediate neighbourhood but should nevertheless be close to public transport routes.

MAIN DESIGN TARGETS

Quality kindergarten environments can be achieved by basing the design on the following features:

- creating environments that allow the staff to focus on caring for and nurturing children. The design should provide features which encourage strong, positive relationships between staff and children.
- trying to imagine how children will use the space, what they will see and what kind of experience they will have, and therefore adjusting the design to their scale.
- responding to local conditions (climate, tradition, design preferences).
- sizing playrooms for the recommended group size according to child supervision ratios.
- using durable and cost effective materials and design details.
- promoting energy efficiency and incorporating other sustainability design features.
- establishing a home-like environment to avoid generating an institutional atmosphere.

LOCATION

Kindergartens are usually located in residential areas to meet the childcare and child education needs of that area. The distance between home and kindergarten should normally be between 500 m and 1000 m and not farther than a 30-minute walk for a 3-year old. Whether a location is appropriate for a new a kindergarten also depends on population growth and how well existing kindergartens service the area.

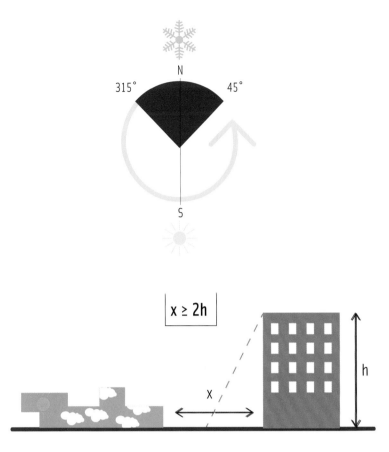

LAND SELECTION CRITERIA

A plot is suitable for a kindergarten if it meets the following criteria:

- quiet zone, away from noise, dust, smoke, industry or major roads
- preferably in a green spot, allowing for the use of green spaces as much as possible
- plenty of sunshine and sheltered from high winds but ventilated at the same time
- not foggy or moist and not situated in the wetlands or floodplains
- not the natural habitat of endangered animal species or protected vegetation
- rational in terms of communications and services to avoid unreasonable costs
- flat terrain or with a minimal southward slope

ORIENTATION

Playrooms in the kindergarten should be positioned so as to enjoy maximum daylight as well as good shading. Playrooms should not face northwards in the range between 315 and 45 degrees, unless such an orientation offers special value, such as a nice view, peacefulness or similar. However, this does not hold for countries with hot climates, where kindergartens should be positioned so as to avoid the sun.

DISTANCE FROM ADJACENT BUILDINGS

In order to generate as much quality space around the kindergarten as possible, especially for play areas, the distance from the kindergarten to each adjacent building should be equal to or greater than twice the height of the adjacent building. This preserves the qualities of the plot as well as well as preventing the kindergarten being overshadowed by neighboring buildings.

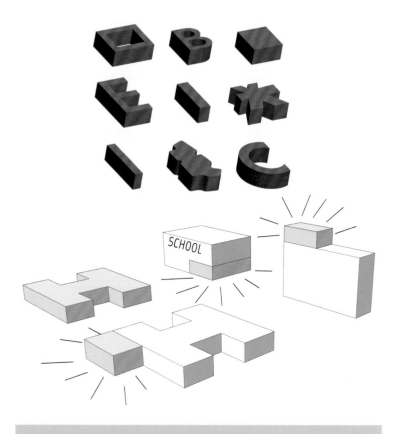

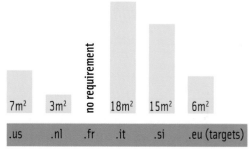

outdoor space per child

7m²	3m²	no requirement	18m²	15m²	6m²
.us	.nl	.fr	.it	.si	.eu (targets)

NO. OF CHILDREN × + = MINIMUM SPATIAL REQUIREMENTS

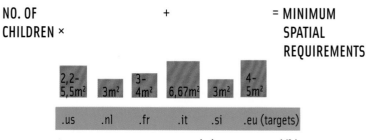

indoor space per child

2,2-5,5m²	3m²	3-4m²	6,67m²	3m²	4-5m²
.us	.nl	.fr	.it	.si	.eu (targets)

Kindergartens exist in various typological forms.

Indoor and outdoor space requirements per child vary from country to country and even between provinces.

TYPOLOGY

Kindergarten typologies are varied, usually responding to the specifics of the location, the typology of traditional construction patterns in the area or special spatial demands. An O-shaped kindergarten, for instance, provides a fully protected internal open air play area, while an E-shaped compound offers half-enclosed patios and direct sunshine from three directions.

There are several types of kindergarten:
- they can be an independent facility,
- a part of another building (e.g. school),
- an extension of another building,
- they can be on the roof of another building, etc.

Traditionally kindergartens have been single storey buildings and many are still built this way today. However, an increasing number of contemporary kindergartens are beign built with several-storeys. This is especially frequent in densely built urban areas and on small plots, where it saves money and space as well as leaving outdoor space for play areas. In multi-storey kindergartens the upper floors are sometimes used for adult spaces only (staff, services), while areas for the children are located on the ground floor.

KINDERGARTEN SIZE

The size of a kindergarten usually depends on the number of children it accommodates. The smallest facilities host two groups of children while the largest can have as many as 12 groups, which means they accommodate between. 40 and 240 children (with an average of 20 children per group). The kindergarten should function as an extension of the home, providing children with sufficient personal attention and a sense of homeliness, which is why smaller kindergartens are preferable to larger ones as they are less likely to be overwhelming for the children and tend to have a less institutional atmosphere. The size of staff and service areas should be in proportion to the size of the children's areas.

SITE SIZE

The size of the site is of special importance, since larger plots give a kindergarten more possibilities for expansion and the introduction of new activities as well as providing additional space for play and learning. The key factor in determining sizes is the number of children the kindergarten is to accommodate, multiplied by the spatial standard, which differs between countries. Countries with dense urban areas usually have more flexible standards and allow for more variation in the size of the site for a kindergarten, stipulating, for example, only the minimum required site size.

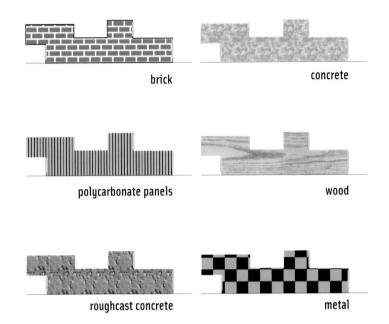

brick

concrete

polycarbonate panels

wood

roughcast concrete

metal

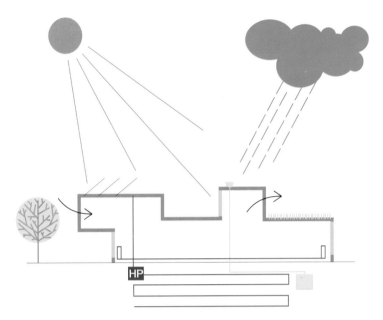

Practically all construction materials are suitable for kindergartens, with wood being especially popular in recent projects.

MATERIALS

The construction of a kindergarten involves the use of a variety of materials, such as wood, brick, concrete and steel, as well as plastics, such as polycarbonate boards. Wood is increasingly being used for construction, in response to eco-friendly construction trends. Materials should be warm and have a pleasant texture for children. For reasons of hygiene materials used to finish the interior should be easy to clean. Quality materials are recommended for their durability, which makes them cost effective in the long-term.

Kindergartens are usually sinlge storey buildings with simple constructions.

CONSTRUCTION

Practically every construction material is suitable: brick, concrete, steel, wood and even plastics (though this latter is rare). The structure should not limit the activities of the kindergarten nor create safety problems. If there are pillars they should be located away from the children's areas or adequately integrated. The building's external shell should be well insulated to protect from inconvenient weather and noise, and its surface should not be rough or rugged so that it does not cause injury to children.

In addition to technical solutions the design of the building itself can promote environmental sustainability. A kindergarten can have various environmentally friendly features.

ENVIRONMENTAL QUALITY

The construction of kindergartens is becoming increasingly sustainable and eco friendly. Here are a few tips on how to get it right:

- **MATERIALS:** Use natural and eco-friendly materials when possible, especially timber.
- **VEGETATION:** Deciduous trees and planting should be empolyed to maximum effect, as they filter the summer sunlight when they are in leaf and allow the sun's rays through in winter.
- **ILLUMINATION:** Well designed openings can provide ample daylight, reducing the need for artificial lighting and thus saving energy.
- **HEATING:** Passive solar heating, solar-thermal panels and geothermal heat pumps are among the renewable energy technologies available for heating the building and generating hot water.
- **RAINWATER:** Collect and use rainwater.
- **BUILDING DESIGN:** Design the building so that it ventilates naturally and is shielded from direct sun in the summer to reduce the need for air-conditioning. Provide children with visual contact with the garden so they learn to appreciate nature and use the building to teach them how to look after the environment (leave natural materials used in the building exposed, teach them to separate waste and recycle, explain what the solar panels on the roof are for, etc).

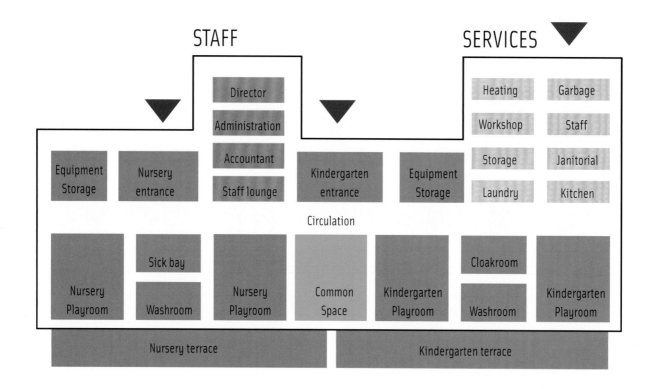

STAFF

SERVICES

Director		Heating	Garbage
Administration		Workshop	Staff
Accountant		Storage	Janitorial
Staff lounge		Laundry	Kitchen

Equipment Storage — Nursery entrance — Kindergarten entrance — Equipment Storage

Circulation

Nursery Playroom — Sick bay — Washroom — Nursery Playroom — Common Space — Kindergarten Playroom — Cloakroom — Washroom — Kindergarten Playroom

Nursery terrace

Kindergarten terrace

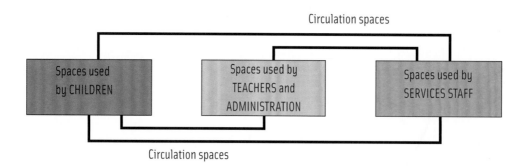

Circulation spaces

Spaces used by CHILDREN — Spaces used by TEACHERS and ADMINISTRATION — Spaces used by SERVICES STAFF

Circulation spaces

INTERIOR SPACES

In the interior a kindergarten is usually divided into three major types of spaces: areas used by children, areas used by the staff and service areas. Children use playrooms and common areas as well as the external playground and circulation paths. It is important to separate children's areas from service areas, such as the kitchen, for health and safety reasons. Sometimes children's areas are kept apart from adult areas by being located in different wings or storeys of the building.

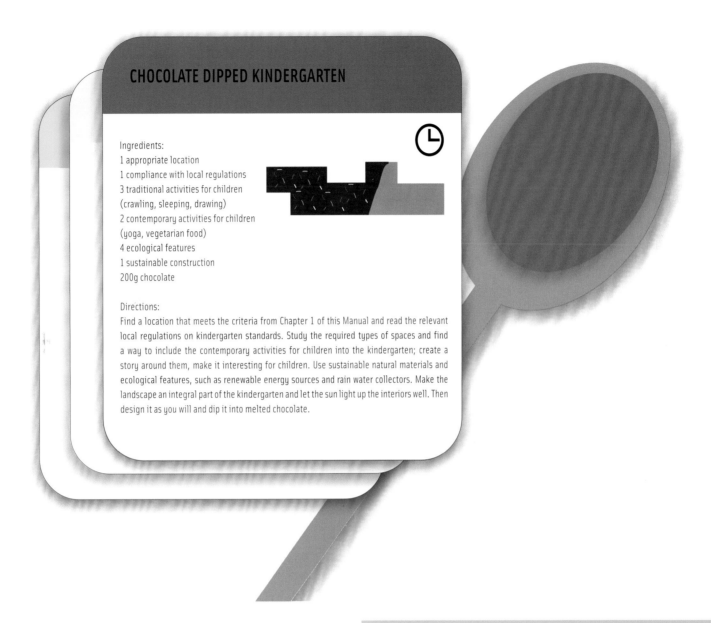

CHOCOLATE DIPPED KINDERGARTEN

Ingredients:
1 appropriate location
1 compliance with local regulations
3 traditional activities for children
(crawling, sleeping, drawing)
2 contemporary activities for children
(yoga, vegetarian food)
4 ecological features
1 sustainable construction
200g chocolate

Directions:
Find a location that meets the criteria from Chapter 1 of this Manual and read the relevant local regulations on kindergarten standards. Study the required types of spaces and find a way to include the contemporary activities for children into the kindergarten; create a story around them, make it interesting for children. Use sustainable natural materials and ecological features, such as renewable energy sources and rain water collectors. Make the landscape an integral part of the kindergarten and let the sun light up the interiors well. Then design it as you will and dip it into melted chocolate.

NEW KINDERGARTEN ARCHITECTURE RECIPE

Kindergartens today are the most exciting they have ever been. Combining diverse spaces and activities such as music, yoga, art, pet care and computer science. It is almost like a small town or an adventure theme park. Designing a kindergarten today means trying to satisfy the needs of contemporary children whilst complying with modern architecture trends. Architects face the challenge of designing kindergartens which, whilst fully complying with all the regulations, have added value and safe and comfortable environments for children.

Kindergarten design is tightly controlled by standards and legislation, which provide the core recipe, but it is architects that add the icing as well as the cherry on top by using clever, child-friendly and innovative solutions.

0-1 INFANTS

1-3 TODDLERS

3+ PRE-SCHOOLERS

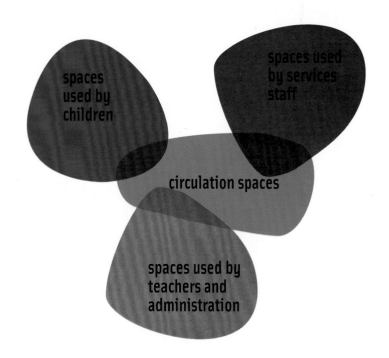

Kindergarten spaces are adjusted to meet the needs of different age groups.

A kindergarten consists of three main types of interior spaces, connected by circulation spaces.

AGE GROUPS

Kindergartens are structured into sections, which are divided into groups of children according to age. These groups are usually for 0–1 year-olds (infants), 1–3 year-olds (toddlers) and 3+ year-olds (pre-schoolers). The smallest children need the most care and attention, therefore their groups are often the smallest. In general, groups of 1–2 year-olds include up to 12 children, groups of 2–3 year-olds have 14–16 children and groups of 4–5 year-olds have 20–25 children. In some countries nurseries for the smallest children are kept separate from facilities for toddlers and pre-schoolers. In this manual we refer to all child care centres for children 0–5 years old as kindergartens.

INTERIOR SPACES

Interior spaces should be designed so as to enable optimum communication among the children and to facilitate their supervision by the staff.

Generally there are three main types of areas in a kindergarten:
a) CHILD AREAS
b) STAFF AREAS
c) SERVICE AREAS

SPACES IN KINDERGARTEN (m²)

No. of groups	2	3	4	5	6
No. of children	44	66	88	110	132
Child areas	190	265	360	438	524
Staff areas	52	52	67	118	118
Service areas	56	66	125	149	163
Circulations	48	63	84	102	123
TOTAL:	346	446	636	807	928

CHILD AREAS (m²)

No. of groups	2	3	4	5	6
No. of children	44	66	88	110	132
Playroom	84	126	168	210	252
Main activity area and sports hall	56	56	75	95	114
Additional activity area	0	16	20	20	30
Child washroom	22	33	40	51	58
Child cloak room	16	24	32	40	48
One-on-one room			8	8	8
Equipment storage	8	8	10	10	10
Outside playground washroom	2	2	4	4	4
TOTAL (m²)	190	265	360	438	524

Areas used by children constitute the largest part of a kindergarten.

a) CHILD AREAS

Every day throughout the year children should be able to engage in a range of activities, both planned and spontaneous. They should be able to play in groups or retire to peaceful nooks and also have the option to be by themselves. Infants need open activity areas where they can crawl, explore, and interact with their teachers; toddlers will run, often in groups; pre-school children need more space and can engage in more sophisticated activities – all this should be considered in designing the interior of a kindergarten.

Children use the following areas:
- playrooms,
- cloakroom,
- activity rooms,
- sports rooms,
- additional activity rooms,
- washrooms,
- terrace or patio,
- circulations,
- external playground.

STAFF AREAS(m²)

No. of groups	2	3	4	5	6
No. of children	44	66	88	110	132
Staff lounge	25	25	35	35	35
External consultant's office	10	10	10	10	10
Resource storage	9	9	9	12	12
Storage for outside play equipment	5	5	10	10	10
Staff washroom	3	3	3	6	6
Director's office				16	16
Administration				12	12
Accounting				9	9
Archive				8	8
Administration washroom				3	3
TOTAL STAFF AREAS:	52	52	67	118	118

SERVICES AREAS(m²)

No. of groups	2	3	4	5	6
No. of children	44	66	88	110	132
Kitchen	40	50	80	100	110
Laundry	12	12	15	15	15
Janitor			8	12	16
Heating/energy room			18	18	18
Toilets	4	4	4	4	4
SERVICES TOTAL (m²):	56	56	125	149	163

b) STAFF AREAS

Staff areas include the director's office, administration and accountancy work spaces, a parent/teacher meeting area, archive room, staff lounge and work area, staff toilet and sometimes a separate room for a nurse. Staff areas are usually located near the main entrance and designed as an independent wing separate from child areas. The size of the staff area depends on the size and type of the kindergarten, and on the number of staff.

c) SERVICE AREAS

A kindergarten requires spaces for a kitchen, food storage areas, a laundry, cleaning cupboards, maintenance areas, a meter room, general storage, and a cloakroom and toilets for service staff. These services are separated from the rest of the kindergarten and have an independent entrance. The size of the service area is in relation to the size of the kindergarten. Cleaning supplies for the kitchen should be kept separate from the equipment for cleaning toilets and other rooms. Children should not have access to the cleaning cupboards.

PLAYROOM

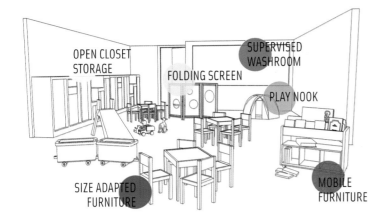

The contemporary kindergarten playroom is a sum of different play spaces.

PLAYROOMS

Children spend most of their day in the playroom, which should therefore be designed to allow for various play and learning areas, and cater for small group, as well as individual, activities while there should also be a group gathering area. Playrooms for infants, toddlers, pre-school children and mixed-age groups of children should be designed for the specific group using the space. Furniture arrangements and constructed elements should be flexible to adjust to age groups or specific activities and learning methods, and there should be nooks where children can be by themselves. Depending on the age group, a playroom will have a play area, storage, a nappy change area, a toilet and hand washing area, sleeping, feeding and food preparation areas.

Regulations on playroom sizes vary between countries and even between provinces. They generally stipulate the minimum floor area per child and not the overall playroom size. Research has shown that children tend to engage in fewer conflicts in larger playrooms.

FURNITURE SELECTION CRITERIA

Kindergarten furniture is appropriate for children if it:

- is adjusted to the age and size of children
- creates variety in the playroom
- is durable
- is safe to use (no sharp edges)
- is easy to clean
- is flexible
- is (preferably) stackable/hangable
- does not create an institutional environment
- makes optimum use of natural materials
- is rich in textures
- is finished in calm, soothing, coordinated colours
- is not too expensive

COLOURS

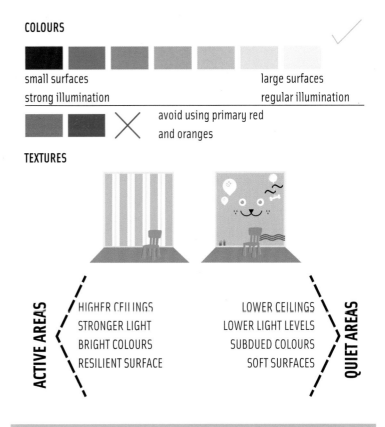

Colour schemes should be adjusted to the size and illumination of spaces. Over-stimulating colours should be avoided.

COLORS

Both color and texture have a great impact on children. Cool colors tend to have a calming effect and warm colors create warmth and excitement. Vivid colors may be applied on one wall in corridors and playrooms, however they should not be overused as this may result in over-stimulated and over-excited behaviour in the children. Primary colors, particularly red and orange, should be avoided. It is better to use too little color in spaces where children spend the majority of their time since their clothing and toys are usually very colorful. Complex patterns are also best avoided. Colors can be used to differentiate areas, such as child areas from staff areas or nap areas from activity areas.

TEXTURES

The sense of touch is very important in cognitive development. Low-lying surfaces should be covered in a variety of textures to stimulate children, especially infants and young toddlers. Soft textures should be used in quiet areas and sleeping areas to promote relaxed and quiet behaviour, while hard textures are well suited for large activity areas.

OTHER ENVIRONMENTAL DESIGN FEATURES

In addition to colour and texture, children's moods can be affected by other elements, such as acoustics, lighting, ceiling height, etc. To stimulate lively motor activities vivid colours and plenty of light should be used, while subdued colors, acoustically absorbant surfaces and lower ceilings tend to have a calming effect on children.

19

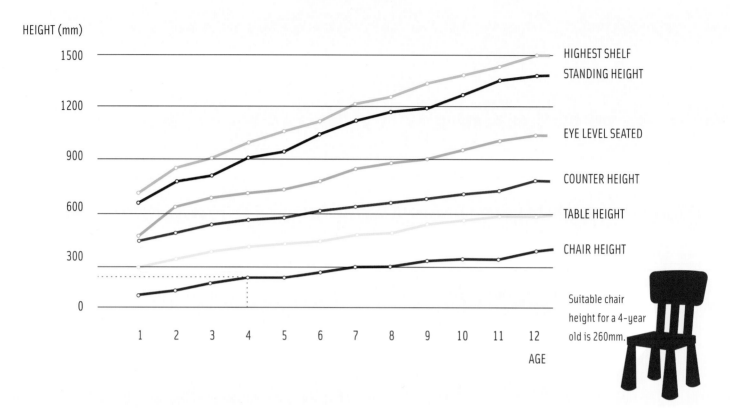

HEIGHT (mm)

1500 — HIGHEST SHELF
      STANDING HEIGHT

1200

      EYE LEVEL SEATED

900

      COUNTER HEIGHT

600   TABLE HEIGHT

300   CHAIR HEIGHT

0

1 2 3 4 5 6 7 8 9 10 11 12

AGE

Suitable chair height for a 4-year old is 260mm.

In designing furniture for children their anthropometric dimensions should be taken into account.

FURNITURE

Playrooms and other spaces for children should be flexible in design so that they can be adjusted for different age groups and learning programmes. Mobile equipment is preferable.

Basic playroom furnishings include:
- tables and chairs, folding beds and other sleeping equipment
- cubby storage for toys, books and children's personal items
- space-shaping elements (shelves, partitions to separate areas)
- bulletin boards, chalk boards
- mirrors
- a table and chair for the teachers
- storage for teaching materials

A playroom for infants should have a feeding area with a nappy storage and nappy change area, and an adult toilet. All furniture elements used to separate areas should allow staff to supervise the entire room. Kindergarten furniture should be certified and compliant with the relevant standards, and all corners should be smooth and round, without sharp edges. Heavy and tall furniture should be fas-tened to the wall or floor for safety reasons. The design of the playroom should be adjusted to the size of the children, including individual elements within the room (doors, windows) and furnishings (chairs, tables, sinks etc).

The above chart gives approximate basic anthropometric data for children of different age groups, which can be used as a guideline for designing custom elements for children.

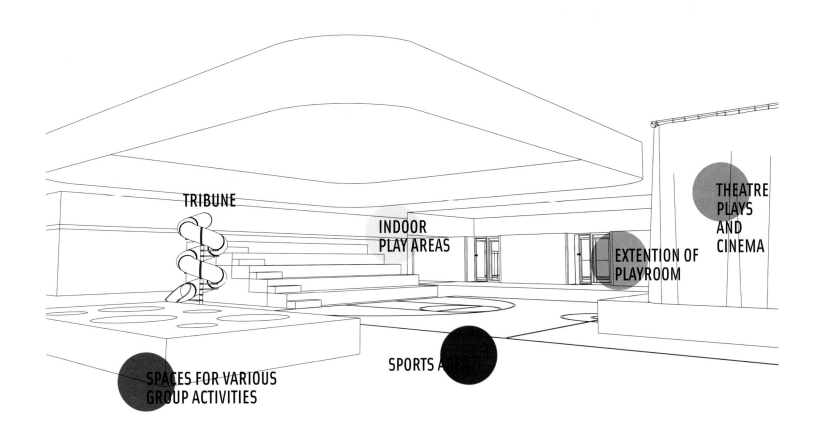

TRIBUNE

INDOOR PLAY AREAS

THEATRE PLAYS AND CINEMA

EXTENTION OF PLAYROOM

SPORTS A...

SPACES FOR VARIOUS GROUP ACTIVITIES

The main activity area is the hub of the kindergarten and can stage various events.

MAIN ACTIVITY AREA

A kindergarten should contain a larger area (> 60 m² (646 sqft)) where children from different age groups can be brought together. It can also be used for sports if the kindergarten has no separate gym. It is recommended that this room have a varied floor plan so that it can accommodate various activities such as puppet shows, group activities, as well as a parents' corner, where parents can talk with each other while waiting for their children. The main kindergarten activity area is increasingly being used by local communities after hours, which contributes to social cohesion.

GYMNASIUM

The gymnasium is a space where children learn to develop their physical skills, coordination and balance. It can be a separate space or part of a larger activities room. Alternatively, if the daycare is close to a school or located inside a school building, the children can use the school´s gymnasium, adapted to the needs of smaller children. If the daycare and the gymnasium are located in different buildings, the distance between them should not be more than 200m (650 ft) or a 5 minute walk.

CLOAKROOMS

This is where children store their outdoor clothing and personal belongings. It is usually located between the entrance and the playroom and consists of storage units for clothes and seating elements, which may be integrated. Each playroom can have its own storage area or there can be a single central storage area island for all groups of children. The storage area for infants and young toddlers should have a nappy change area and sink. Each child should have a storage area at least 200 mm (8 in) in length. Children should be able to mark their cloakroom section unambiguously or have lockers.

ENTRANCE

The entrance of the daycare should be easily accessible and visible, and located away from busy streets. An overhang covering the entrance or a lobby is generally a good idea, to protect parents and children from inclement weather. Dropping off and picking up children should be as uncomplicated as possible, and staff should have a separate entrance from the parents and children. In general, there should be an entrance for every 2–4 play areas of the facility.

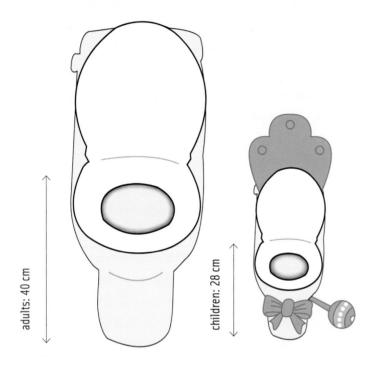

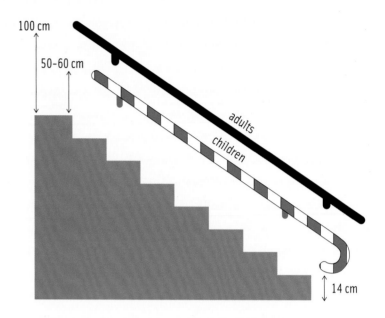

adults: 40 cm

children: 28 cm

100 cm

50-60 cm

adults

children

14 cm

> The main elements should be adjusted to children's dimensions.

WASHROOMS

Washrooms should be adjusted to age groups. Older toddlers use potties, either in the washrooms or a section of the playroom. Toilet areas are to have gates at the entrance and may have child-height partitions between booths (recommended min. booth size is 1,100 x 800 mm (3 ft 7 in x 2 ft 7 in). Doors should not have locks and should open outwards. Hinges should be protected so that small fingers cannot become trapped in them. The toilet booth partitions must allow supervision. Pre-school children must be provided with separate facilities for boys and girls when more than one toilet is provided. These facilities should be accessible from the classroom and must have doors for privacy. Washrooms must be finished in materials that can be easily disinfected and cleaned with common cleaning products. Steel elements must be specified in stainless steel. Glazed ceramic tiles are recommended both for the floors and walls up to at least 1 m (3 ft). It is convenient for washrooms to be shared by two adjacent playrooms in order to optimize costs and space.

COVERED TERRACES

The covered terrace is an extension of the playroom and provides children with a play and learning area partially protected from the weather. In sunny areas it offers shade. For small children terraces should be fenced with non climbable fences at least 600 mm (2 ft) high. Various materials can be used for the terrace roof which should be designed such that it does not reduce the amount of daylight in the interior. Covered terraces generally begin at around 15 m² (160 sqft) .

STAIRCASES

Staircases for children should be adapted to their size. The depth (D) to height (H) ratio of each step is defined as 2H + D = 610 mm (24 in), with the recommended height of the risers being 140 mm (5 1/2 in). Treads must have non-slip surfaces that can be cleaned with liquids and disinfected. Step edges should be rounded. Gaps between balusters must be smaller than or equal to 85 mm (3 5/16 in) or they should be replaced by a single protective element. The handrail should be at a height of 1 m (3 ft) for adults and 500 – 600 mm (1 ft 8 in - 2 ft) for children. The handrail for children should fit the size of their hand. The accessibility of the kindergarten should conform with local regulations and legislation.

COMMUNICATIONS

Corridors should be short and can accommodate various programmes, such as children's art gallery. The pathway between the kitchen and playrooms should have no obstacles to aid in manipulating food cart traffic. If the kitchen and playrooms are on different levels, a lift is required to deliver food.

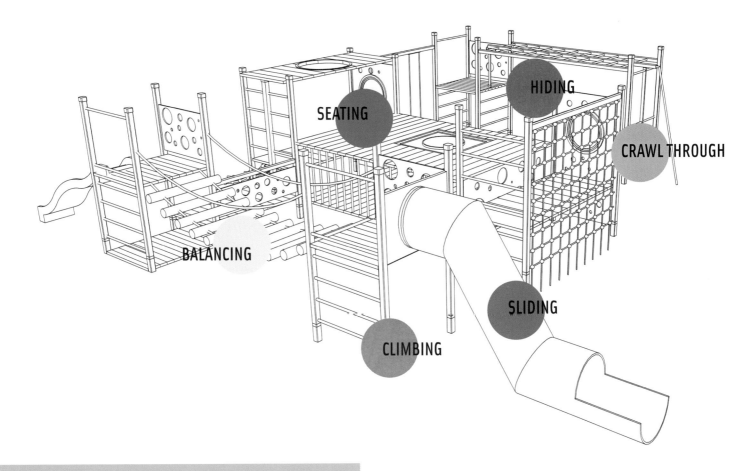

SEATING

HIDING

CRAWL THROUGH

BALANCING

SLIDING

CLIMBING

The open-air playground is an extension of the playroom and promotes motor development. It should be as diverse as possible.

PLAYGROUNDS

The external playground is an extension of inside play areas and should provide children with a variety of activities appropriate to their stage of development and the teaching curriculum, giving them the opportunity to socialize or enjoy privacy. It should offer a minimum of 15 m² (160 sqft) per child except in cases where there are green areas in the immediate surroundings that children can use safely, in which cases less playground space can be provided. Simple combination play structures should be provided to support various activity types (sand/water play, climbing, toys with wheels, etc). Preferably there should be separate play areas for each age group or alternatively the play equipment should be arranged such that toddlers and pre-school children can play side by side. The ground surfaces should be diverse. Pathways and natural surfaces should account for at least a half of the playground and part of it must be covered in non-slip surfaces (e.g. asphalt, plastics, etc). If there is a staircase in the playground it should be clearly marked, and if it has more than three risers it should have a hand rail. The playground should have storage for outside play equipment, and a water fountain.

Location

The playground should be in a sunny spot, sheltered from wind, with natural shade as well as additional shading elements. There should be non-poisonous shrubs or plants in the playground.

Safety

The playground must be enclosed by a fence to define the play area, allow ease of supervision and protect children from strangers or stray animals. The fence should be non-climbable and at least 1.20 m (4 ft) high. It should appear light but can be covered by vegetation, such as a hedge, on the inside or outside. If there is a dangerous area nearby (water, etc), the fence should bend inwards at the top. Fence gates should close automatically, and the handles should prevent children from being able to open them from the inside.

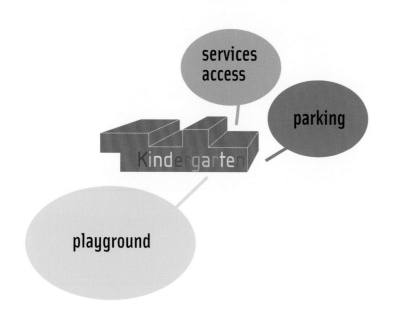

artificial

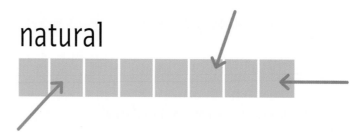

500 lx work surface / reading / close work

300 lx ambient light for class and play areas

Lighting intensities should range from 500 lux in areas for activities with close detail to 50 lux in sleeping and napping areas.

natural

Sufficient window openings, preferably from several directions.

The kindergarten's exterior spaces include a playground with natural surfaces, services access areas and a parking area. They should be designed in line with their function.

It is important to design the kindergarten so as to use as much natural light as available. Daylight saves energy, floods the interior with light and brings children into contact with nature.

PARKING

Parking should be provided for staff as well as drop-off areas for parents to use when they bring or collect their children, in which case the parking time should also allow for brief conversations with teachers. Parking for the disabled should also be provided. The parking area should never be arranged in a way that forces children or wheelchair users to pass behind parked cars. Walkways in front of parking spaces must be protected to prevent vehicles from advancing into the walkway zones. The parking area should be located away from busy intersections but preferably close to bus and transport stops, and it should provide secure bicycle parking. A general guideline is to provide two parking spaces for each group of children.

SERVICES ACCESS AREA

This is where service personnel deliver food and supplies and waste is collected. It should be located next to service areas, away from the main entry and separated from children's activity areas.

LIGHTING

All rooms used by children and those used by staff should have abundant natural light. Playrooms should preferably face South to allow children to enjoy the maximum amount and warmth of light during the entire day. The window surface area in playrooms should be equal to 20 per cent of the floor area. To prevent the back of the playroom being too dark, the distance from a window to the back wall should not be greater than 2.5 times the distance from the floor to the top of the window, otherwise the room should have windows on two sides, which is recommendable in any case. It is important to have window openings at child height, to allow visual contact with the exterior. Visual continuities should also be generated within the kindergarten, between playrooms and between playrooms and circulation spaces.

Artificial lighting can be used to emphasize areas, mark boundaries, evoke feelings or cause a desired response. Most appropriate for large motor activity spaces is medium intensity lighting (250 lx), while manipulative activities (reading, painting and close work) require task lighting (500 lx), and quiet and sleeping areas need lower light levels (50 lx). 100 lx is acceptable for circulation spaces. Light levels in all rooms must allow visual observation of from adjacent spaces. Reflective surfaces should be avoided. Lamps must have shatterproof lenses or covers and be fixed in place. Children must be prevented from coming into direct visual contact with the light source. Adequate exterior lighting should be provided to allow safe exterior circulation and for site security.

COLD   COOL   WARM   HOT

Winter: 21°C; 35% min. relative humidity
Summer: 24-26°C, 50% max. relative humidity

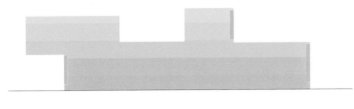

NATURAL VENTILATION

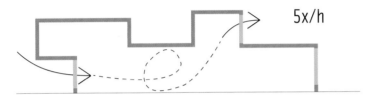

5x/h

The kindergarten must be designed to function as a child's second home, and it must be heated and ventilated appropriately.

Safety: the most important word in a kindergarten. Spaces must be carefully designed to enable safe and fun play and learning.

HEATING/VENTILATION/AIR-CONDITIONING

Temperature control is very important in a kindergarten, and particularly so at floor level since children spend a great deal of time on the floor. The recommended air temperature and humidity ranges are 21°C (70°F) with 35 percent minimum relative humidity for wintertime and 24–26°C (75 - 79°F) with 50 percent maximum relative humidity during summertime, whereby infants may be more comfortable in a somewhat warmer atmosphere than older children. The interior should be well ventilated, either manually (windows) or mechanically. Air should in the playrooms should be renovated at least once every hour, however drafts and cold air should be avoided. Air conditioning is recommended in high temperature environments provided it is set to a temperature suitable for children. Fans should not be used; if they cannot be avoided, they must be out of reach of the children and cleaned weekly.

SAFETY

Safety is the single most important factor in kindergarten design and planning and should always come first. Children are unpredictable and like to explore, which they must be able to do in a safe environment. All situations and design solutions that could pose a safety threat for the children should be eliminated in the early planning stages. Safety standards for kindergartens, including fire safety, evacuation and other considerations, are usually stipulated in national or local building regulations for public buildings or are defined in related regulations (e.g. for furniture).

BIBLIOGRAPHY

This manual has been compiled with reference to kindergarten standards and legislation from the USA, the European Union, France, Croatia, Slovenia, Austria, Spain and Venezuela. The following publications are some of the most comprehensive on the subject:

- General Services Administration (GSA): Child Care Center Design Guide (2003): Public Buildings Service Office of Child Care, Washington
- Pravilnik o normativih in minimalnih tehničnih pogojih za prostor in opremo vrtca (2000): Uradni list Republike Slovenije, Ljubljana
- Auf-Franič H. (2003): Dječje jaslice i vrtići: upute za programiranje, planiranje i projektiranje, Arhitektonski fakultet Zagreb, Zagreb
- Morss P. et al. (2005): Children in Europe, Issue 8, Children in Scotland, Edinburgh

ecosistema urbano

Ecopolis Plaza

Madrid, Spain

Photographs: Emilio Doiztua, Javier de Paz

The project "Plaza Ecopolis" aims to incorporate the idea of sustainability into daily life. The main focus is therefore to create a vision of urban sustainability that facilitates the reduction of energy consumption through its design, but that also aims at raising people's awareness of their own consumption behavior. The layout of the building generates a public space that can be used by the area's residents. The space has been treated as an "open environmental classroom", an integrated educational program for children aimed at improving the urban environment. The Madrid-based studio ecosistema urbano believes that projects such as "Plaza Ecopolis" are a way to impart awareness of sustainability to children, who consequently will become responsible adults.

The technologies used for the Ecopolis project minimize the consumption of both energy and natural resources. Once consumption was dramatically reduced, the designers analyzed the use of active systems based on alternative energies.

A complete energy simulation study was developed by the Thermodynamics Research Group at the Industrial Engineering School of Seville. This simulation study was the key to understanding the behavior of the building and helped to select the best location for each and every constructive element. Decisions such as that of half burying a large amount of the building (50% of the building takes advantage of the land's thermal inertia) or including a large south-facing glass façade shaped the physical relationship between the building and its environment. A bioclimatic textile layer superimposed over a light steel structure wraps the rational concrete core of the building. This textile, which is partially movable and adjusts to the sun's position through sensors, is the interface between interior and exterior spaces, blurring the boundaries between the private and public realms and extending the inner comfort to the outdoor space.

The building extends its limits into the plaza and part of its functional processes are placed outside to make them more transparent to the public, again raising awareness regarding the management of natural resources. The sewage system ends in a lagoon in front of the building where all the waste water from the building is naturally purified by macrophyte plants. All the purified water is stored underground in a gravel tank and is used for all the irrigation needs of the plaza. This artificial landscape emulates a natural riverbank.

Architecture:
ecosistema urbano

Project team:
Belinda Tato, Jose Luis Vallejo,
Michael Moradiellos, Domenico di Siena,
Jaime Eizaguirre, Ion Cuervas-Mons,
Luisa Zancada, Benjamín Castro,
Masatoshi Oka, Johannes Kettler,
Javier de Paz, Julia Casado, Álvaro Ferrer,
Emilio García, Andrea Franceschi,
Ioannes Busca, Pau Munar, Ignacio Cabezas

Water purification system:
Diego Hurtado

Energy concept:
Thermodynamics Research Group at the
Industrial Engineering School of Seville

Facilities engineering:
Julio Bernal

Structural engineering:
Juan Rey, Rinske Daniels

Lighting consultant:
Targetti Poulsen, Juan José García

Textile engineering:
BAT spain

Client:
Rivas Vaciamadrid Town Council

Built area:
3,000 sqm (32,291 sqft)

An artificial topography has been created as an enclosure and protection filter from the aggressive industrial environment. Within the plaza it is easy to forget about the context and to imagine you are somewhere else, closer to nature.

Site plan

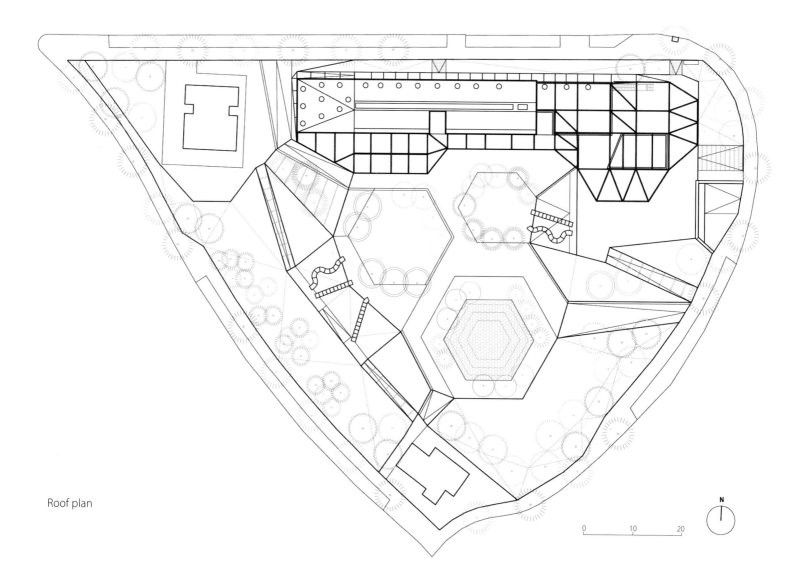

Roof plan

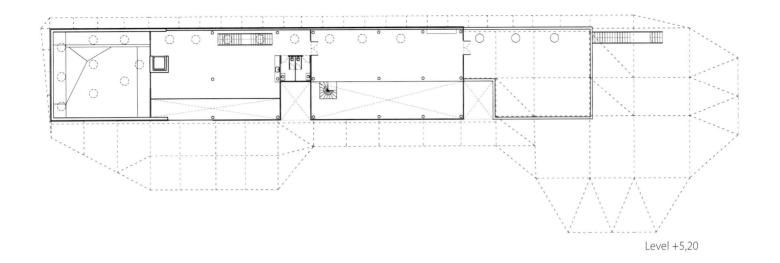

Level +5,20

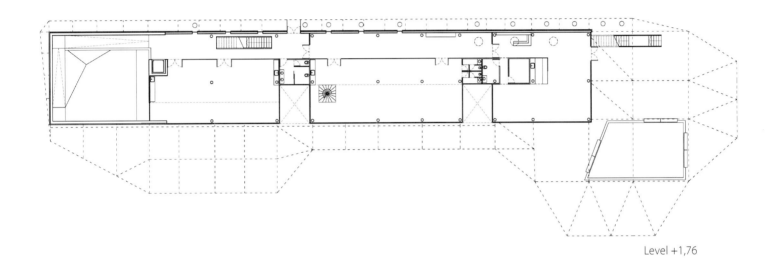

Level +1,76

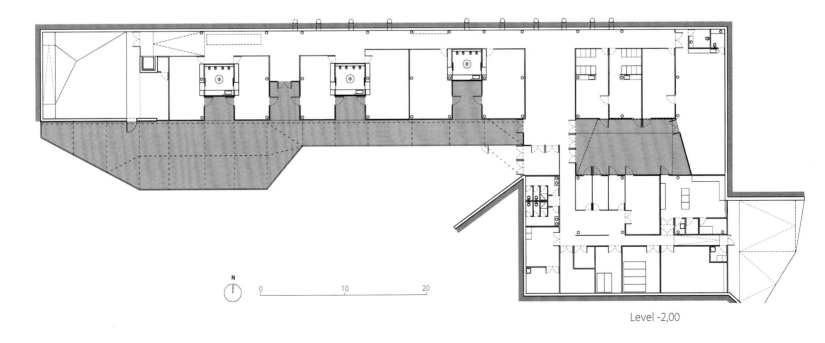

N

0   10   20

Level -2,00

29

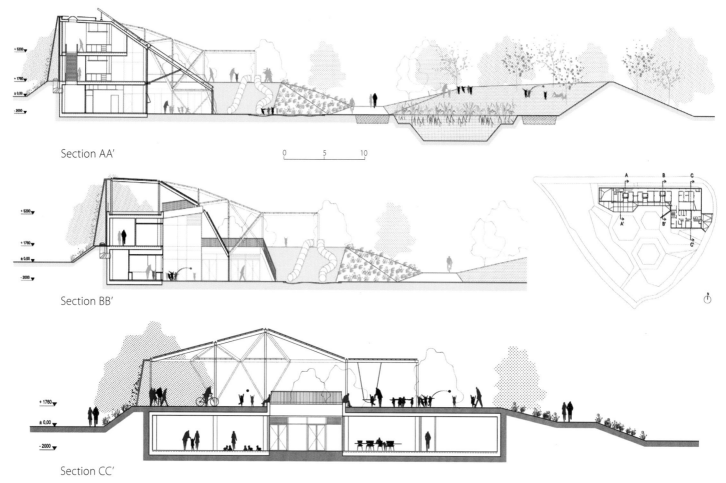

Section AA'

0 5 10

Section BB'

Section CC'

© Emilio Doiztua

© Emilio Doiztua

30

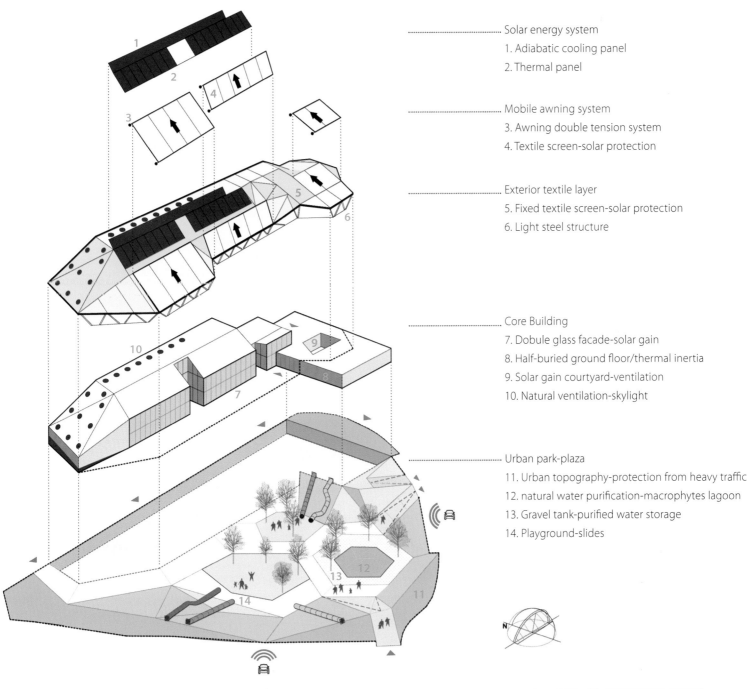

Solar energy system
1. Adiabatic cooling panel
2. Thermal panel

Mobile awning system
3. Awning double tension system
4. Textile screen-solar protection

Exterior textile layer
5. Fixed textile screen-solar protection
6. Light steel structure

Core Building
7. Dobule glass facade-solar gain
8. Half-buried ground floor/thermal inertia
9. Solar gain courtyard-ventilation
10. Natural ventilation-skylight

Urban park-plaza
11. Urban topography-protection from heavy traffic
12. natural water purification-macrophytes lagoon
13. Gravel tank-purified water storage
14. Playground-slides

© Emilio Doiztua

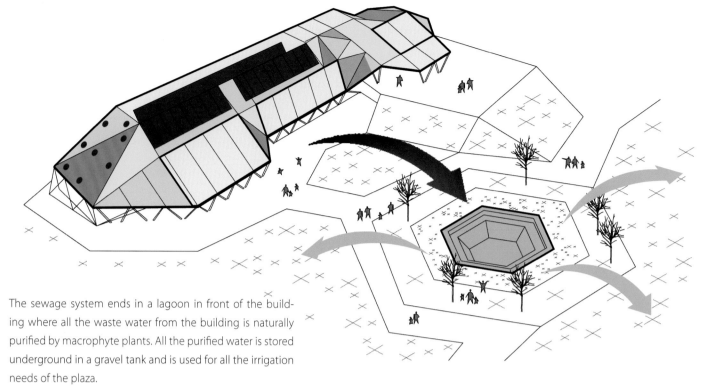

The sewage system ends in a lagoon in front of the building where all the waste water from the building is naturally purified by macrophyte plants. All the purified water is stored underground in a gravel tank and is used for all the irrigation needs of the plaza.

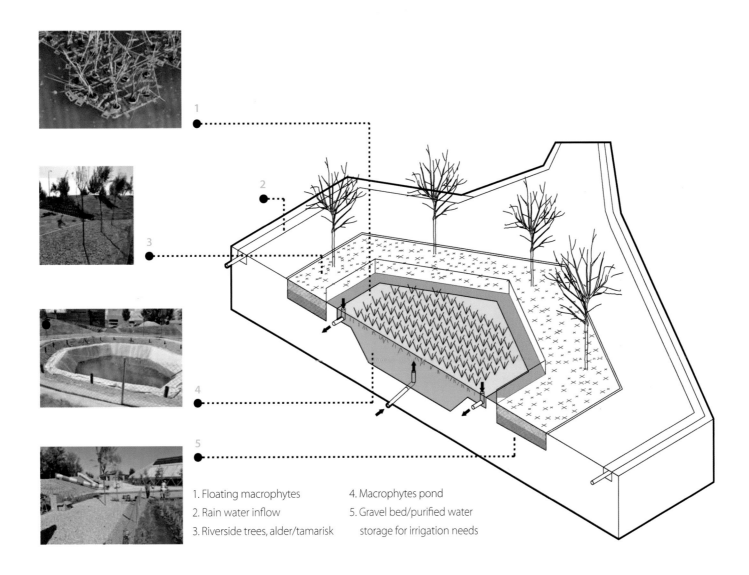

1. Floating macrophytes
2. Rain water inflow
3. Riverside trees, alder/tamarisk

4. Macrophytes pond
5. Gravel bed/purified water
   storage for irrigation needs

HIDROLUTION SYSTEM FMF
(floating macrophytes filter),
circulation diagram

1. Waste water
2. Screening + water mixing + pumping
3. Rain water
4. Inflow
5. Recirculation

6. Gravel bed, purified water storage
7. Macrophytes pond
8. Recirculation pump
9. Outflow
10. Green areas

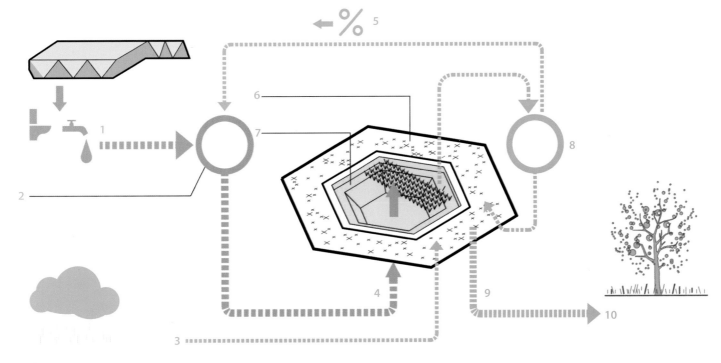

A bioclimatic textile layer superimposed over a light steel structure wraps the rational concrete core of the building. This envelope is partially movable and adjusts to the sun's position through sensors. It is the interface between interior and exterior spaces, blurring the boundaries between the private and public realms and extending the inner comfort to the outdoor space.

© Javier de Paz

© Javier de Paz

© Emilio Doiztua

© Emilio Doiztua

© Emilio Doiztua

© Javier de Paz

© Emilio Doiztua

© Javier de Paz

© Emilio Doiztua

© Emilio Doiztua

© Emilio Doiztua

© Javier de Paz

38

Decisions such as that of half burying a large amount of the building or including a large south-facing glass façade shaped the physical relationship between the building and its environment.

Reiulf Ramstad Architects

Fagerborg Kindergarten

Oslo, Norway **Photographs:** Thomas Björnflaten, Søren Harder Nielsen, RRA

Reiulf Ramstad Architects have designed a new kindergarten and accompanying outdoor facilities for Fagerborg Congregation in central Oslo An existing nursery and a park of standard were removed to make room for the Fagerborg Kindergarten. Consisting of 2 units for children between 1-3 years old and 2 units for children between 3-6 years old, the gross building area is around 1200 sqm (13,000 sqft)

There were many cultural heritage guidelines to be considered in the project site. As a requirement from the local authority, the kindergarten had to have a contemporary expression. With its location in the middle of a small city park, the kindergarten essentially had a protected garden as an outdoor area. The 4 kindergarten units function both independently and together as required, sharing a common area and kitchen in the heart of the building. Administration is placed on the upper floor separate from children areas.

As in nature, where seeds need the best soil to flourish, children, the "Citizens of Tomorrow," need stimulation in their everyday sphere. While kindergartens often display pedestrian materials and poor architectural design, the Faberborg Project prioritized developing a building with a rich architectural register that would form an important first phase outside the family in the environment of the future generation.

A review from trendhunter.com says of the kindergarten that "the gorgeous Norwegian landscape and the pure minds of impressionable children are catered to in the Fagerborg Kindergarten by Reiulf Ramstad Architects. The elementary ... takes on a truly organic aesthetic thanks to the natural wood employed in its construction."

The building is contemporary, yet designed so as not to feel out of place among the other buildings in the area, most dating between 1900 and 1950. The timber exterior reflects Norway's cultural heritage, yet the building is thoroughly modern, with the façade tapering sharply on one side, so that the building seems to lift off from the entrance.

The interior is bright, flooded with natural light, cheerful and colorful.

Architecture:
Reiulf Ramstad Architects
Client:
Fagerborg Congregation
Area:
1,200 sqm (13,000 sqft)

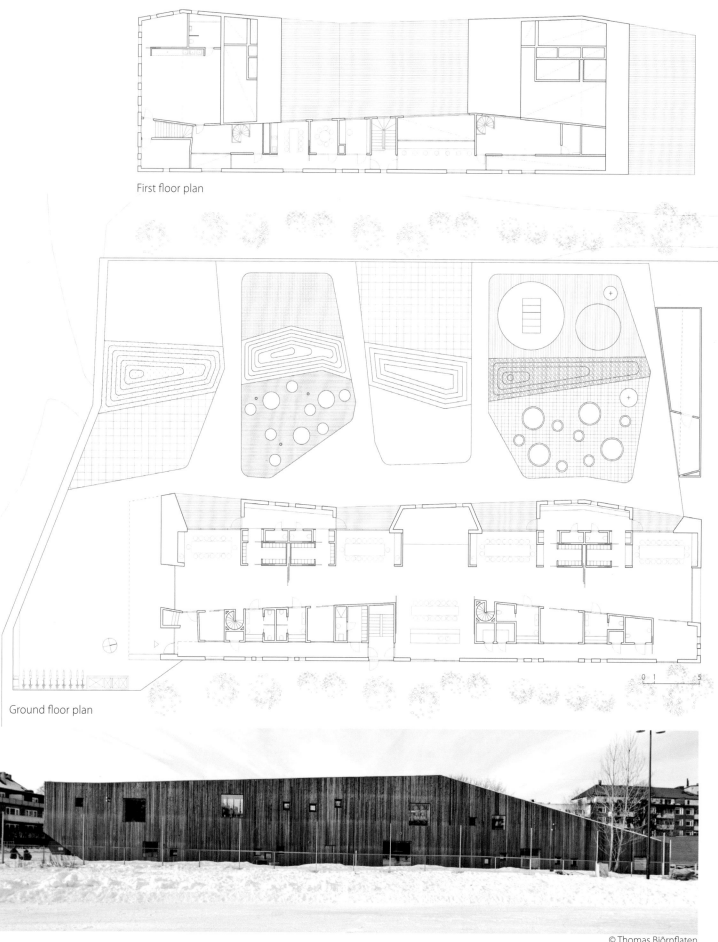

First floor plan

Ground floor plan

0 1   5

© Thomas Björnflaten

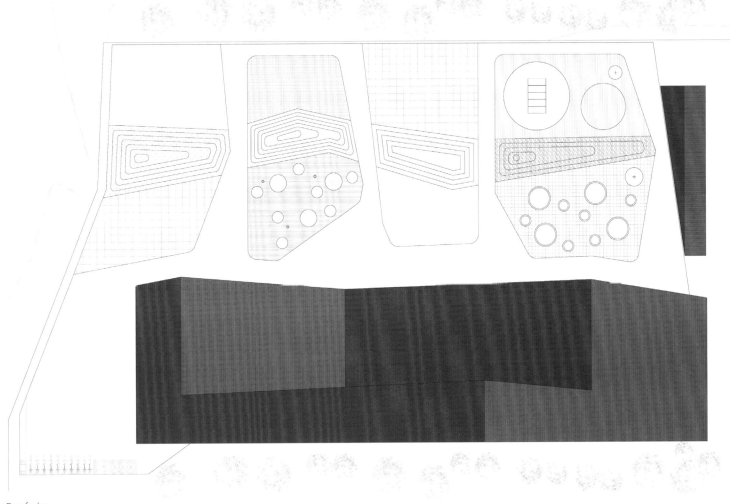

Roof plan

43

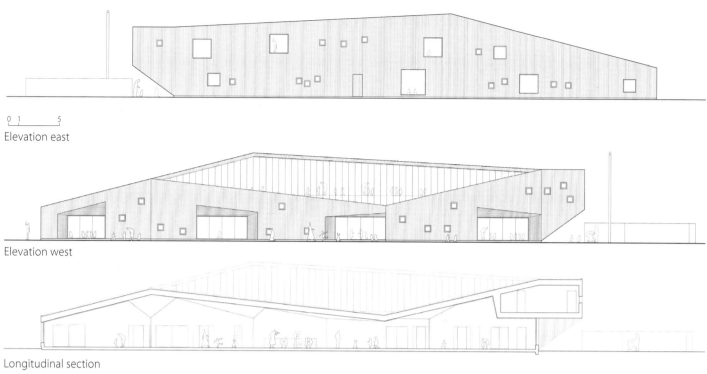

0 1 5

Elevation east

Elevation west

Longitudinal section

© RRA

© Søren Harder Nielsen

© Thomas Björnflaten

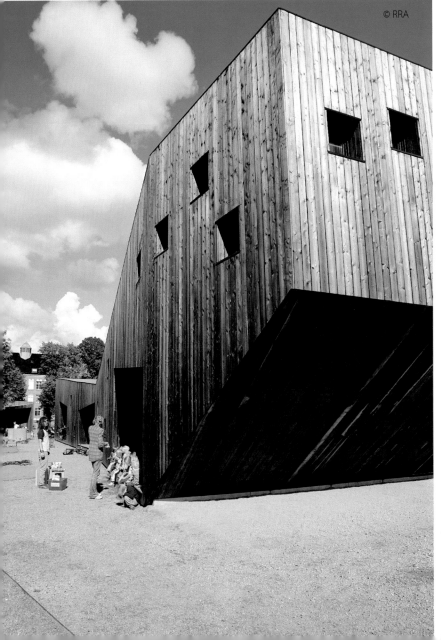

© Thomas Björnflaten

The building is contemporary, yet designed so as not to feel out of place among the other buildings in the area, most dating between 1900 and 1950. The timber exterior reflects Norway's cultural heritage, yet the building is thoroughly modern, with the façade tapering sharply on one side, so that the building seems to lift off from the entrance.

© RRA

© Thomas Björnflaten

There were many cultural heritage guidelines to be considered in the project site. The area is characterized by residential buildings from 1900-1950; however, as a requirement from the local authority, the kindergarten had to have a contemporary expression.

© RRA

© Søren Harder Nielsen

© RRA

While kindergartens often display pedestrian materials and poor architectural design, the Faberborg Project prioritized developing a building with a rich architectural register that would form an important first phase outside the family in the environment of the future generation.

© Thomas Björnflaten

© Thomas Björnflaten

© Thomas Björnflaten

The interior is bright, flooded with natural light, cheerful and colourful.

© Søren Harder Nielsen

© Thomas Björnflaten

© Thomas Björnflaten

Christensen and Co. Architects

Sunhouse – Climate Friendly Nursery

Horsholm, Denmark

Photographs: Adam Moerk

The nursery is built on 'Active House' principles and is yet another example of how considered architectural design and integrated energy technologies create a recipe for sustainable architecture.

The geometry, the position of windows and a range of state of the art green technologies contribute to a compact and climate-friendly building. Designed as a triangle, the two longest façades face south east and south west, where windows and roof lights allow more than three times as much light to enter as in a standard building. This ensures a healthy indoor climate year round.

The purely architectural solutions – the form of the building and the choice of materials including high performance glass and generous amounts of insulation – ensure that even without any high-tech renewable technologies the building will use less energy than the requirements set by the 2015 Danish building regulations. But the nursery has also been equipped with a series of renewable technologies to enhance its performance even further. Strategically positioned on the southern façades of the roof are 50 sqm (500 sqft) of solar collectors providing heating and hot water (backed up by a heat pump), and 250 sqm (2,700 sqft) of photovoltaic panels to generate electricity.

When not used for solar panels the remaining roof surface has been planted with sedum, a hard wearing plant, which encourages biodiversity, prevents water runoff and provides sound and temperature insulation. Water evaporating from the planted roof helps to cool the photovoltaic panels, which work more efficiently at lower temperatures. It's a simple, effective and attractive solution.

The choice of concrete for the floor and walls of the structure further optimize the performance of the building, as the material has a high thermal massing, meaning that solar energy streaming in during the day is absorbed by the walls and floors and then gradually released as the inside temperature cools in the late afternoon and evening. Concrete does require a lot of energy to create, but its capacity to absorb heat and its durability make it a good choice over the life time of the building. The exterior of the building is clad in Superwood timber, a product that is treated with high pressure rather than toxic chemicals.

In total the nursery produces 8 kilowatt hours per sqm per year, which is surplus to the building's requirements. This means that during eight months of the year excess energy is fed back into the national grid and for the four darkest months of the year, renewable energy is bought back by the nursery. The outdoor areas are planted to represent the various landscapes of Denmark, including a woodland area and a sandy zone to symbolize the coastline, as well as on-site greenhouses, where staff will help the children grow plants and vegetables. It has also been designed to educate its young users about protecting the environment; rainwater is collected for watering the plants, helping to teach the children about reusing and recycling natural resources.

The shed housing the various toys, tools and bicycles is equipped with outdoor pedals, the children then have to collaborate in producing the energy for the shed, in order to turn the lights on.

The design team has, throughout the design process, used sophisticated software to evaluate the design of the building. These virtual tests have resulted in subsequent improvement of the energy performance, indoor air quality and daylight levels.

Architecture:
Christensen and Co. Architects,
Hellerup Byg (Contractor),
Ramboll DK (Engineers)
Client:
Horsholm Municipality, Denmark,
VKR Holding, Lions Children House
Area:
1,300 sqm (14,000 sqft)

Designed as a triangle, the two longest façades face south east and south west, where windows and roof lights allow more than three times as much light to enter as in a standard building. This ensures a healthy indoor climate year round.

N

Site plan

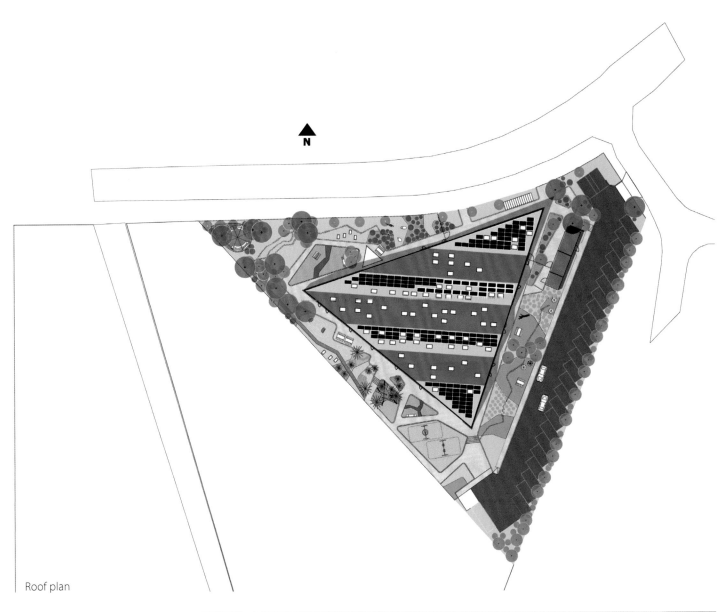

Roof plan

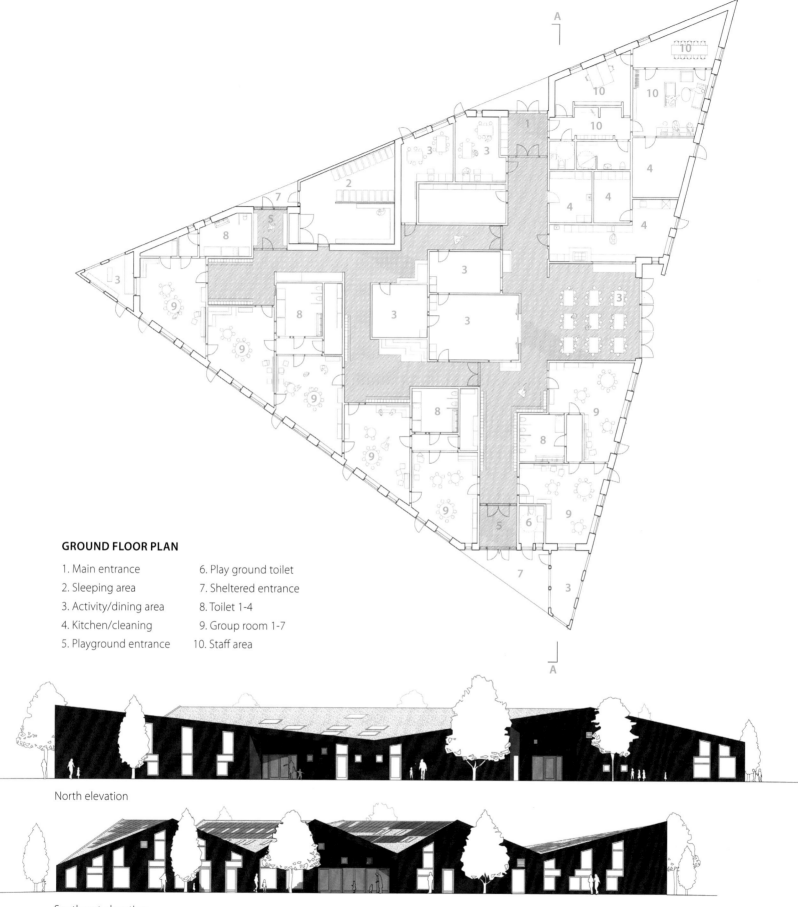

GROUND FLOOR PLAN

1. Main entrance
2. Sleeping area
3. Activity/dining area
4. Kitchen/cleaning
5. Playground entrance
6. Play ground toilet
7. Sheltered entrance
8. Toilet 1-4
9. Group room 1-7
10. Staff area

North elevation

Southeast elevation

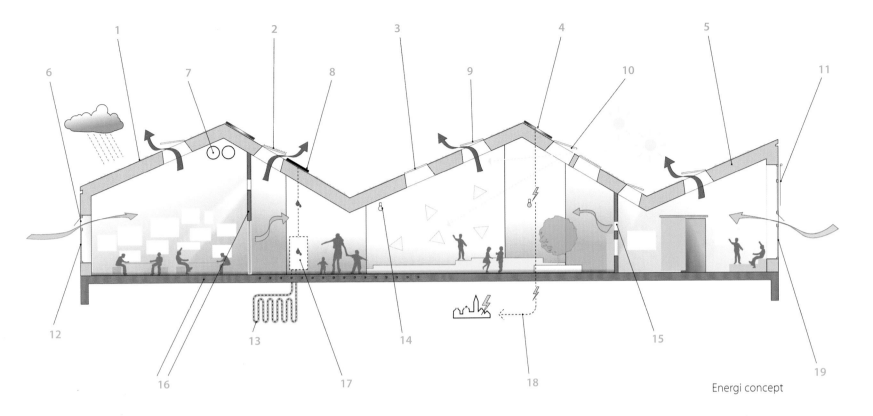

Energi concept

1. Sedum roof, has cooling effect in micro climate (up to 3ºC reduction of surrounding temperature) and prevents flooding of drainage by retention and subsequent slow release of rain water

2. Solar screening (roof), integrated in all south facing roof windows-solar powered

3. North facing roof windows contributes with diffuse daylight and ventilation

4. Photovoltaic strips at roof ridge, where the structure doesn't allow for windows

5. Building envelope with high performance, high density insulation

6. Fresh air inlet via façade windows

7. Mechnical ventilation, pipes with large diameter, counterflow and heat recovery unit

8. Solar panels placed on south facing roof surface near plant room

9. Natural ventilation via "chimney effect". All roof windows are opened according to requirement and controlled by WindowMaster

10. South facing roof windows optimized angle on roof allow maximum daylight and passive solar heating even in season with low sun position

11. Solar screening with automated solar screens above child reach. Solar powered

12. More closed north façade, heat loss is minimized via fewer openings. 3-layer thermal glazing is used for optimised window energy efficiency and lifespan

13. Daily and seasonal storage short term solar heat storage in water tank. Long term solar heat storage in geothermal system

14. Lighting, zoned lighting with low energy and LED fittings

15. Cross ventilation controlled passage of fresh air through internal walls

16. Thermal mass, concrete floors and walls stabalize temperatures due to the material's high thermal inertia

17. Solar complete heat system, heat from solar panels and heat pump used for water and heating

18. Solar energy, power from roof used in building and surplus is "stored" in local power grid

19. Open south façade, maximised usage of daylight and solar heating. 2-layer thermal glazing is used for optimised window energy efficiency and lifespan

Section AA

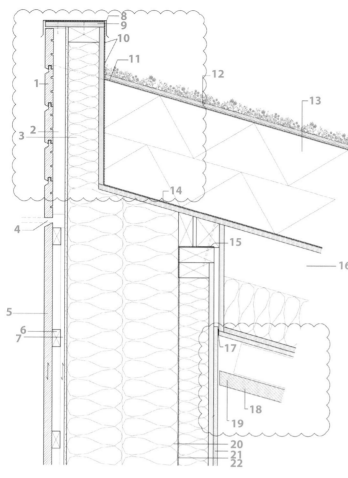

1. Wood Cladding (superwood profile type AART 5"), angled as the roof slope
2. Ventilated Opening
3. Pre. fab lightweight insulated wall panels, 95/435 mm insulation
4. Ventilated opening
5. Horizontal wood cladding (superwood profile type AART 5")
6. 25 mm Vertical distance batten
7. 12 mm Horizontal distance batten
8. Zinc flashing
9. 15 mm plywood
10. 2 Layers Roof membrane
11. 2 Layers Roof membrane
12. Sedum
13. 300 mm insulation (rigid)
14. Vapor Barrier
15. Joint Filler (airtight)
16. Pre. fab lightweight insulated roof panels, 145 mm insulation
17. Joint Filler (airtight)
18. Acoustics ceiling, ink. 100 mm steel framing
19. Acoustics ceiling (finale detailing is done at the site)
20. Pre. fab lightweight insulated wall panels
21. 1 Layer 12 mm plywood and 1. Layer 12,5 mm plasterboard
22. Vapor BarrierX

Roof detail

58

Arhitektura Jure Kotnik

Kindergarten Ajda 2

Ravne na Koroškem, Slovenia

Photographs: Miran Kambič

Kindergarten Ajda is the extension of a kindergarten in Ravne na Koroškem, a small town in northern Slovenia. It has replaced a former temporary kindergarten extension, which was set up from three containers and had one playroom, offering at the time immediate relief for lack of kindergarten space. To create a permanent extension, thirteen 20' ISO containers were added to the three existing ones and all of them carefully incorporated into a unique whole. Ajda's containers are arranged into clusters and joined by a single roof, with spaces in between used for various purposes such as dressing room, covered terraces and multi-purpose entrance.

Ajda consists of a total of 16 containers, which host three classrooms, two covered terraces and two washrooms for children, all of them dynamically connected with the dressing room and multi-purpose entrance hall. The interior is not only spacious but very bright, since the playrooms' longer walls are fully glazed to enable children good visual communication with the green surroundings. The spacious multi-purpose entrance hall functions as a gallery for children's artwork, play area and reading nook, and is equipped with a mobile theater screen. One corner of the kindergarten was made into roofed open-air terraces in teak wood, allowing for the children to play outside well protected from weather inconveniences all year round.

The signature design feature of kindergarten Ajda is its didactic façade, made from thick anthracite isolative and fire-resistant boards covered in colorful magnets of five colors. The lightweight magnets are foldable so that children can manipulate them with ease, combining colorful design blocks to create animals, vehicles, buildings and other imaginary shapes. The interactive façade helps improve children's motor skills, eye-hand coordination and problem-solving techniques, as well as stimulates creativity and encourages the matching of colours, shapes and sizes.

Architecture:
Arhitektura Jure Kotnik
Collaborators:
Andrej Kotnik, Tjaša Mavrič, Tina Marn
Client:
Municipality Ravne na Koroskem
Area:
450 sqm (4,800 sqft)

1. Playroom 1
2. Toilet 1
3. Toilet 2
4. Playroom 2
5. Terrace 1
6. Playroom 3
7. Terrace 2

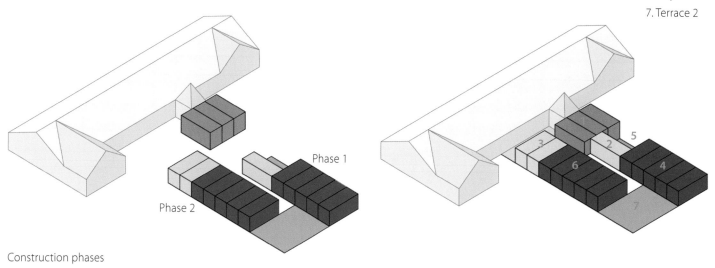

Phase 1

Phase 2

Construction phases

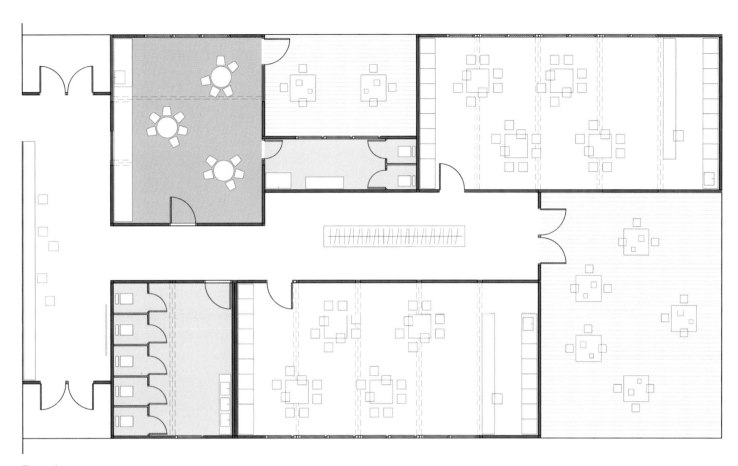

Floor plan

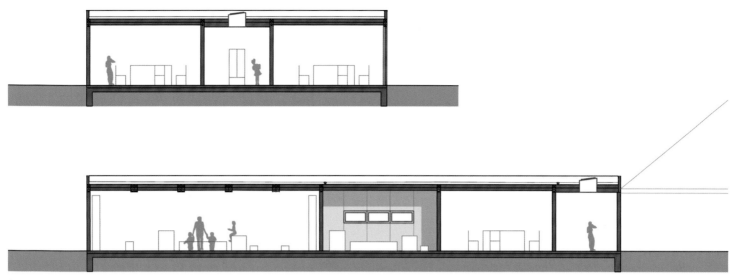

Sections

Magnets

The signature design feature of kindergarten Ajda is its didactic façade, made from thick anthracite isolative and fire-resistant boards covered in colorful magnets of five colors. The lightweight magnets are foldable so that children can manipulate them with ease, combining colorful design blocks to create animals, vehicles, buildings and other imaginary shapes.

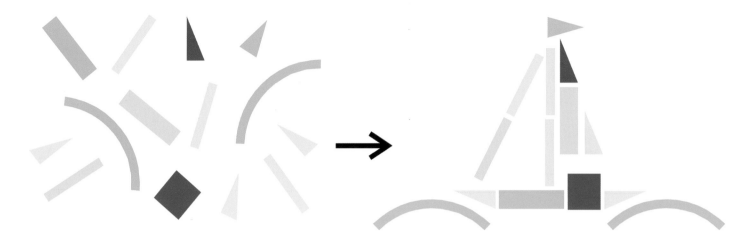

Kindergarten Ajda's magnetic façade:

1. Is a toy that allows children to arrange magnets into various shapes, such as animals, vehicles, buildings and imaginative designs;

2. Helps children develop problem-solving skills, creativity , sort relationships, as well as match colors, shapes and sizes;

3. Helps improve eye-hand coordination and motor coordination;

4. Enhances children's creativity and intelligence, their IQ and EQ;

5. Is a didactic tool for teachers and can support the learning process;

6. Is a design novelty that combines interest, benefit and creativity

Kirsch ZT GmbH

A Loft For Children

Vienna, Austria

Photographs: Hertha Hurnaus

This nursery, occupying a compact two-story building, offers a distinctive identity in a heterogeneous urban environment and blends harmoniously with its surroundings. The rectangular core is designed as a spatially open system. A "filter layer" consisting of secondary rooms, outer stairs and a patio area with plants for shade from the sun and secure play areas mediates between interior and exterior space. Exciting insights and views are created by open and closed façade elements.

The twin concepts of functional openness and spatial intimacy were important in the nursery's design. In addition to the administration, a therapy room and a bistro, the ground floor houses two group rooms for toddlers. The corridor between the rooms is used as a play and communication area between the groups. The play berths were designed to be spatially differentiated and provide the children with opportunities for recreation, but also for retreat and relaxation.

Following the wishes of the client, a large open space was designed on the first floor, which is easily divided into play areas and areas for creative projects. The flexible furniture was specially designed to complement the space and to provide the children with different options for combination. In this way, room and area are created and recreated time and again. The group rooms on this level also have play berths. The secondary rooms are designed as annexes, resulting in an unusual and exciting façade structure.

Due to the short construction period (six months), the design chosen had to be easily assembled; in the end it is a composite construction of in-situ concrete and prefabricated wooden elements. The two-story nursery, which consists of the central structure and the secondary rooms as annexes, is built on a reinforced concrete slab with a circumferential ice wall. The main structure has two different ceiling systems. The ceiling above the ground floor is a massive in-situ concrete ceiling (h = 28 cm), the wooden beamed ceiling (h = 12.5 cm) above the first floor rests on a joist support system.

The additional rooms are made of laminated timber and are horizontally connected to the main body. The building is braced via a central core of reinforced concrete.

The nursery was designed as a passive house construction. An air-water heat pump was installed on the flat roof for the required heating load. During the summer months, support cooling via the ventilation system is provided through the heat pump. The minimum required hygienic change of air is ensured by a ventilation system with heat recovery and summer bypass. The climate control of the entire building during the summer occurs through the ventilation system by cooling the incoming air, and the passive house construction ensures the residual heat supply during the operating time via the ventilation system.

Architecture:
Kirsch ZT GmbH
Selection method:
1st prize, EU-wide, open competition
Project manager:
DI Hannah Feigl
Static constructive supervision:
Werkraum Wien ZT Gmbh
HVAC, sanitary and electrical planning:
Bauklimatik Gmbh Wien,
Technisches Büro Braun
Open space planning:
Rajek Barosch Landschaftsarchitektur
General contractor:
Pittel & Brausewetter
Timber structure:
Kaufmann Bausysteme
Client:
City of Vienna
Gross floor area:
1,200 sqm (12,900 sqft)
Covered area 830 sqm (8,900 sqft)

Ground floor plan

0   5   10

First floor plan

The twin concepts of functional openness and spatial intimacy were important in the nursery's design.

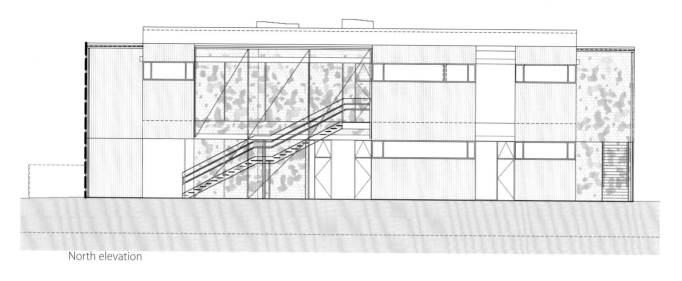

North elevation

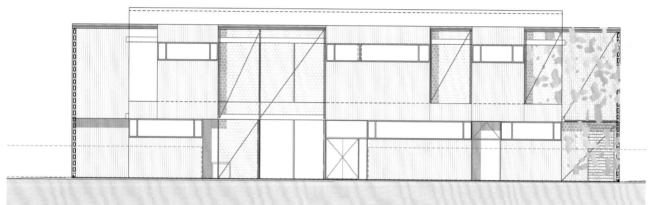

West elevation

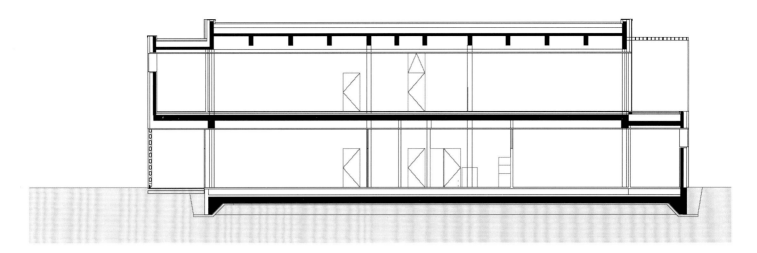

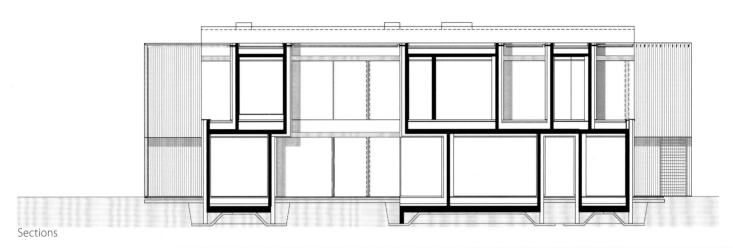

Sections

The flexible furniture was specially designed to complement the space and to provide the children with different options for combination. In this way, room and area are created and recreated time and again. The climate control of the entire building during the summer occurs through the ventilation system by cooling the incoming air, and the passive house construction ensures the residual heat supply during the operating time via the ventilation system.

DETALLE DE FACHADA

1. Safety overflow
2. Metal sheet
3. Anti-insect protection
4. Bracket
5. IPE beam 160/82/60 mm
6. Z-shaped profil 30/130/30/4 mm powder-coated
7. Horizontal slats for solar protection
8. Insulation
9. Oak lintel, 80 x 160 mm
10. 1 cm board
11. Doorjamb, 60 x 160 mm
12. Sheet connecting pillar and wooden beam
13. Facilities strip
14. Oak profile, 80 x 160 mm
15. Girder
16. Rockwool
17. Insulation glass
18. Removable grille 150 mm
19. Prefabricated concrete support
20. Steel sheet, e = 8 mm
21. Drain filter
22. Asphalt
23. Water collecting duct

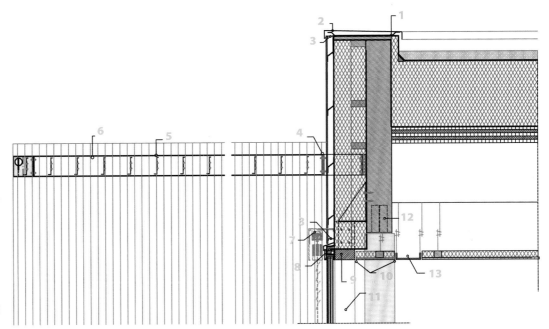

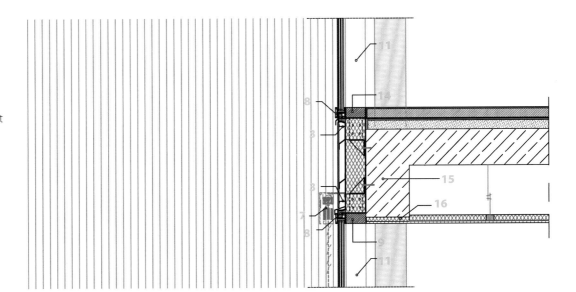

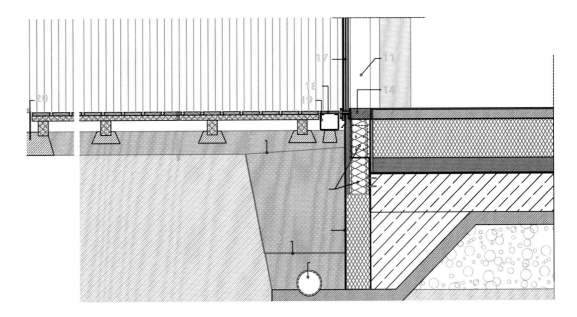

Ecker Architekten

Kindergarten Dandelion Clock

Buchen/Odenwald, Germany

Photographs: Constantin Meyer

The project brief set out by the Neckar-Odenwald County required an economical structure that could be built quickly. The Dandelion Clock kindergarten educates 38 physically or developmentally challenged children. The building comprises four modules, each of which contains two group classrooms and a small therapy room. Large roof overhangs above all the terraces provide the building with "intelligent" solar shading in the summer months and allow "solar gain" in the winter. They also enable the children to play outside on the terraces even in bad weather.

The units are radially distributed around an atrium, which is the largest single space in the school. This flexible meeting room serves as a circulation zone, an indoor playing field, a communal dining hall, and the place where all the children begin and end their school day. The size of the atrium also permits joint group activities and celebrations, fulfilling a vital part of the school's educational mission which was originally thought to be beyond the budget of the project.

The center is naturally illuminated and ventilated by four prominent roof monitors which form what is known as the "jester's cap". Opening lower vents in the classroom façade and the window flaps mounted at the top each monitor draws air through the entire building, cooling the space during warmer days or when the atrium is densely populated without the need for mechanical air-conditioning. Excess warmth is ventilated through a "thermal chimney" in the "jester's cap" above the atrium. The monitors form the visual identity of the kindergarten, which has a strong presence despite sprawling, commercial surroundings. The cladding of these elements in standing-seam gold-anodized aluminum roofing creates an important point of pride for the children who are schooled here.

The entire building is a wooden frame construction, with glue-laminated timber columns and beams. Connection reveals in the timbers, designed to accept aluminum curtain wall profiles, were milled with a CNC wood router in the carpenter's shop to ensure precision on the construction site. The almost identical building modules enabled factory production of large framed panels. Exterior walls are clad with robust, painted clapboard andprotection for the laminated timber construction is provided by aluminum roof edging and window cladding.

Wood also plays a dominant role in the interior design, with visible glue-laminated beams and columns, and general wall surfaces built from OSB (oriented strand-board) and Fermacell (a gypsum and wood-fiber dry-walling) and then painted. The color concept for the interior decoration reinforces the radial form of the building and assists in the spatial orientation of the children educated here. The built-in cabinetry is made from MDF with a plastic laminate surfacing, and the custom children's tables are oak surfaced with desk-top linoleum. Solid-core doors with opalescent plastic laminate surfacing and solid wood edging are finished with stainless steel hardware. Linoleum flooring is used throughout the building. The hung ceilings are Heraklith, a magnesite-cement and wood-fiber acoustic panel, and insulation in the ceilings and walls is provided by blown-in loose-fill dry cellulose. The construction period for this building, from groundbreaking to ribbon-cutting, was a mere 8 months.

Architecture:
Ecker Architekten
Structural engineering:
Färber + Hollerbach
Environmental engineering:
Ingenieurbüro Willhaug
Carpentry:
Zimmerei Bechtold
Client:
Neckar-Odenwald County
Represented by County
Executive Dr. Achim Brötel

The building comprises four modules, each of which contains two group classrooms and a small therapy room. The units are radially distributed around an atrium, which is the largest single space in the school.

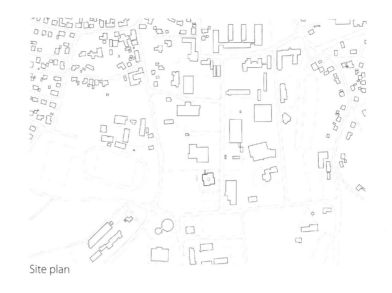

Site plan

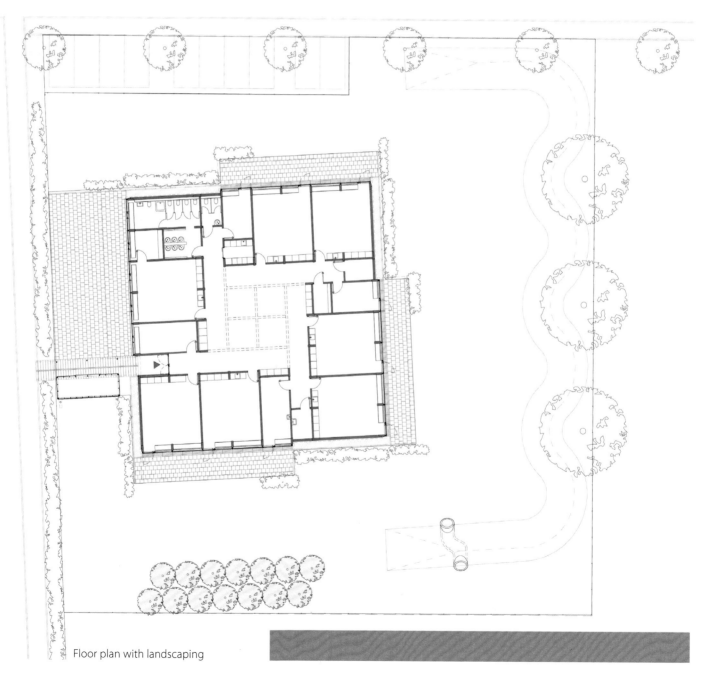

Floor plan with landscaping

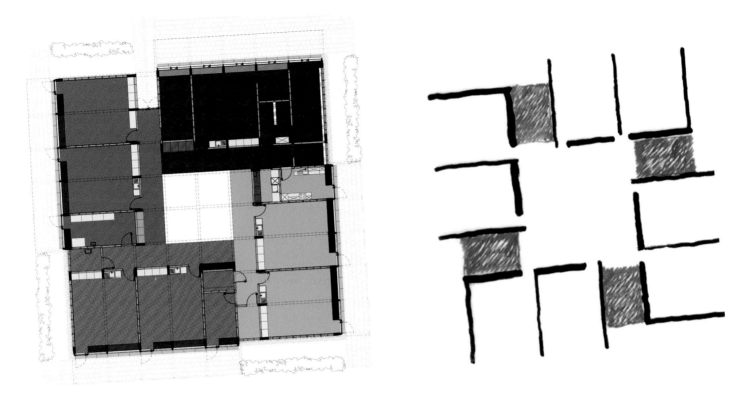

Clock color concept

Concept sketch

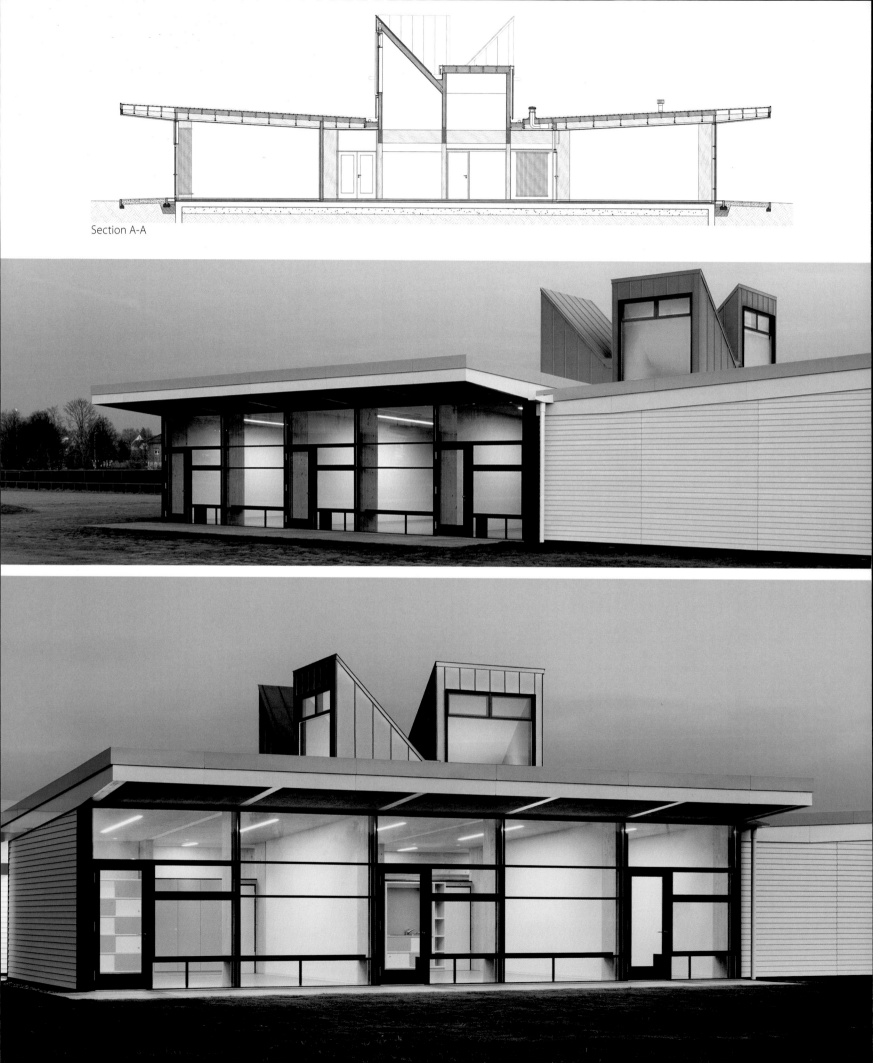

Section A-A

Section C-C

The color concept for the interior decoration reinforces the radial form of the building and assists in the spatial orientation of the children educated here.

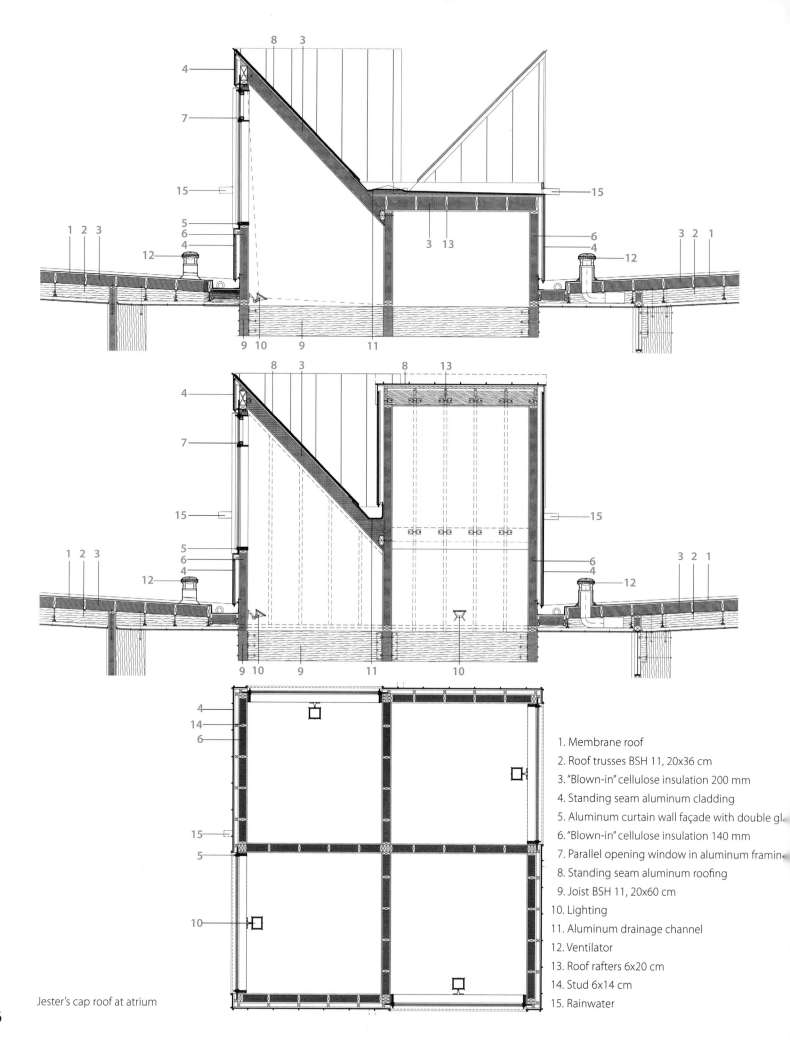

Jester's cap roof at atrium

1. Membrane roof
2. Roof trusses BSH 11, 20x36 cm
3. "Blown-in" cellulose insulation 200 mm
4. Standing seam aluminum cladding
5. Aluminum curtain wall façade with double gl.
6. "Blown-in" cellulose insulation 140 mm
7. Parallel opening window in aluminum framin
8. Standing seam aluminum roofing
9. Joist BSH 11, 20x60 cm
10. Lighting
11. Aluminum drainage channel
12. Ventilator
13. Roof rafters 6x20 cm
14. Stud 6x14 cm
15. Rainwater

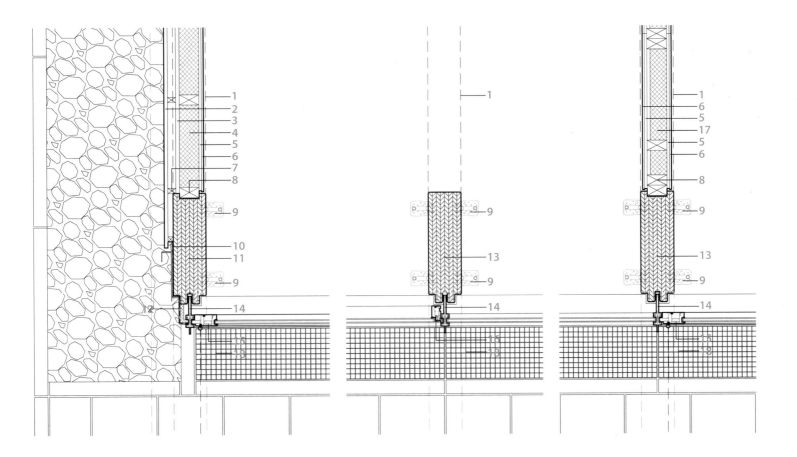

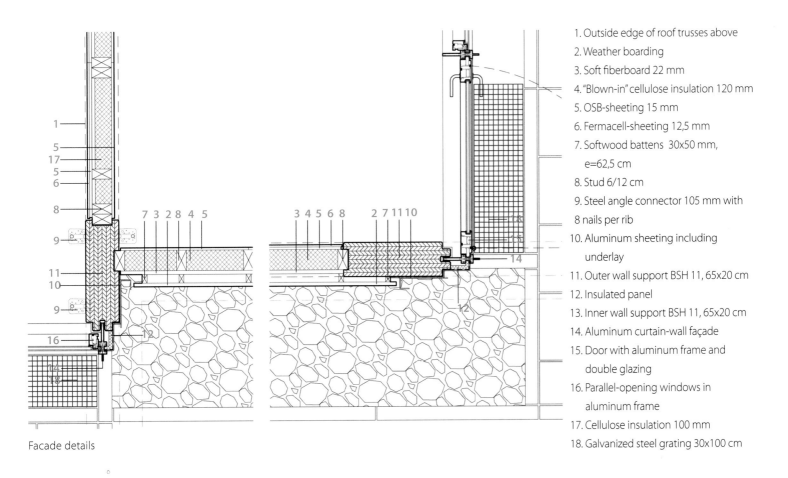

Facade details

1. Outside edge of roof trusses above

2. Weather boarding

3. Soft fiberboard 22 mm

4. "Blown-in" cellulose insulation 120 mm

5. OSB-sheeting 15 mm

6. Fermacell-sheeting 12,5 mm

7. Softwood battens 30x50 mm,
   e=62,5 cm

8. Stud 6/12 cm

9. Steel angle connector 105 mm with
   8 nails per rib

10. Aluminum sheeting including
    underlay

11. Outer wall support BSH 11, 65x20 cm

12. Insulated panel

13. Inner wall support BSH 11, 65x20 cm

14. Aluminum curtain-wall façade

15. Door with aluminum frame and
    double glazing

16. Parallel-opening windows in
    aluminum frame

17. Cellulose insulation 100 mm

18. Galvanized steel grating 30x100 cm

Batlle i Roig arquitectes

Nursery in the Málaga Gardens in Barcelona

Barcelona, Spain

Photographs: contributed by Batlle i Roig arquitectes

The redesign of the Malaga gardens, located in the interior of the block bound by Nicaragua, Berlin, and Numancia streets and Avenue Josep Tarradellas in Barcelona, promoted the allocation of a small site for the construction of an education facility: a nursery. The rectangular shaped site is attached to a dividing wall. One of its long sides closes off the interior of the block, and faces the gardens of the courtyard.

The small area of the site prevented the program from being developed with only a single story, though this would have been desirable. In the end it was organized on two floors, which allowed all the classrooms to face south. The need for playgrounds and porches on both levels was solved with a structural offset in section. The classroom access, on both levels, is through a wide corridor lit by a patio attached to the neighboring division wall. The entrance, located at one end of the volume, was protected by another offset of the upper volume that created a cantilever over the access.

The play of volumes and geometries imposed on the building by the small area of the site was softened by the choice of materials; concrete for the structural elements for the less sunny side façades, and metal, both opaque and perforated, on the sunnier ones. In the interior, this monolithic appearance of the building was solved by the use of materials with a better tactile quality such as wood and rubber, and by the chromatic color palette.

The lush vegetation of the garden, in addition to the plants which will soon be blooming on the patios of the nursery, shelter this small building, visually confusing the interior and exterior, but welcoming and protecting the little inhabitants.

Architecture:
Batlle i Roig arquitectes
Collaborators:
Laura Quintana, Goretti Guillén,
Arantxa Manrique, architects,
Francesc Parera, draftsman
Developer:
Consorci d'Educació de Barcelona
(Barcelona Board of Education)
Construction Company:
CGN /construc-green ingeniería y servicios, sl
Surface:
700 sqm (7,500 sqft)

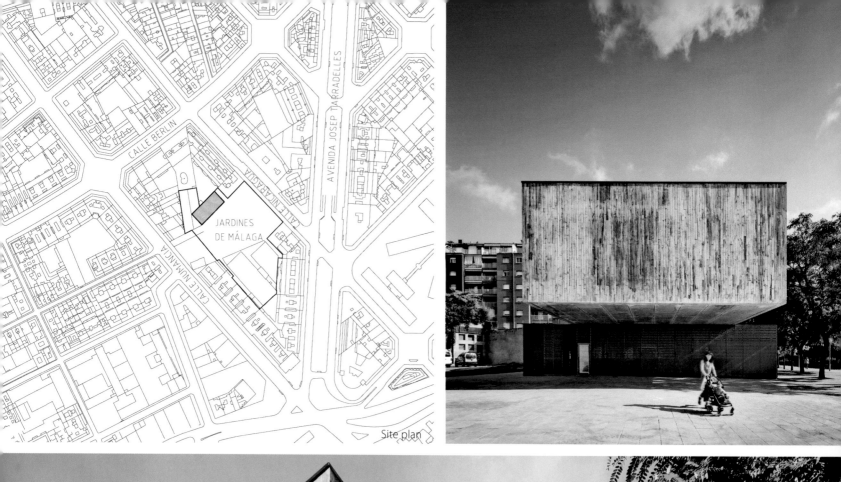

Site plan

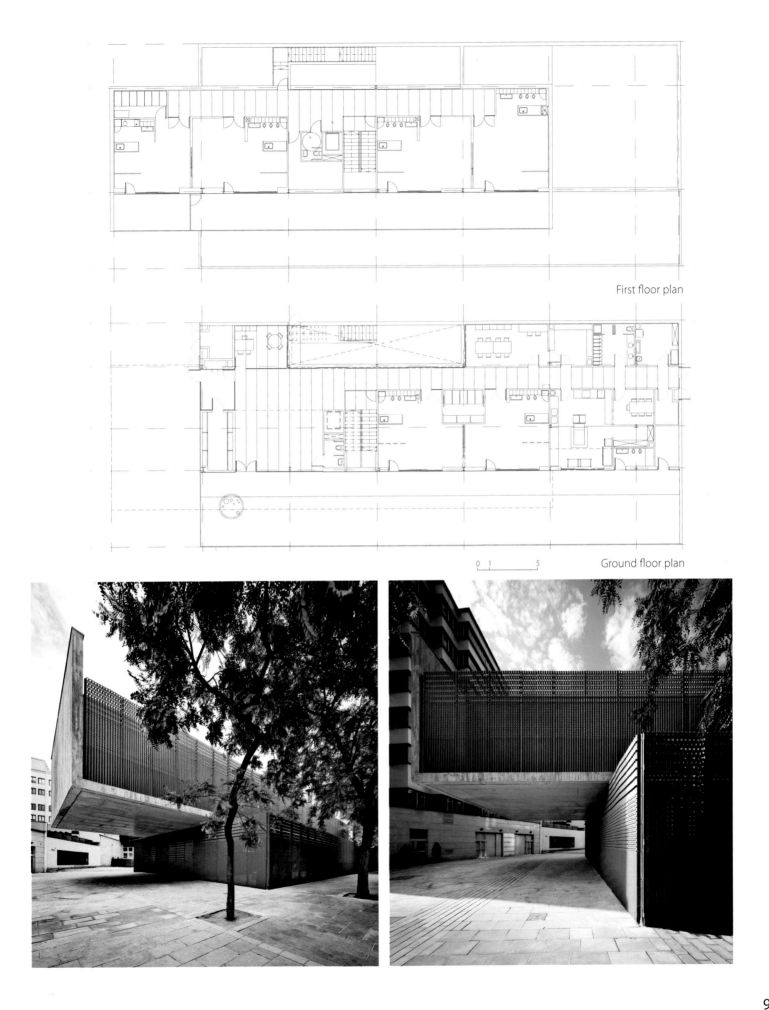

First floor plan

0 1   5   Ground floor plan

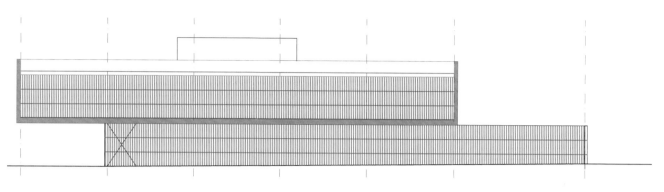

Garden elevation

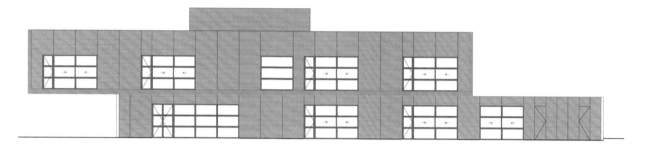

Interior elevation

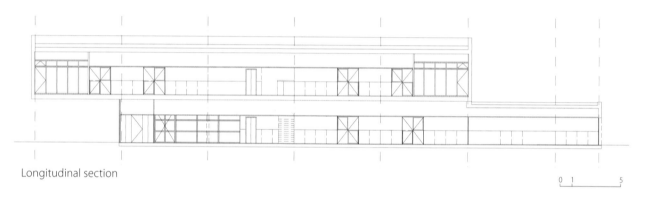

Longitudinal section

0   1   5

The play of volumes and geometries imposed on the building by the small area of the site was softened by the choice of materials; concrete for the structural elements for the less sunny side façades, and metal, both opaque and perforated, on the sunnier ones.

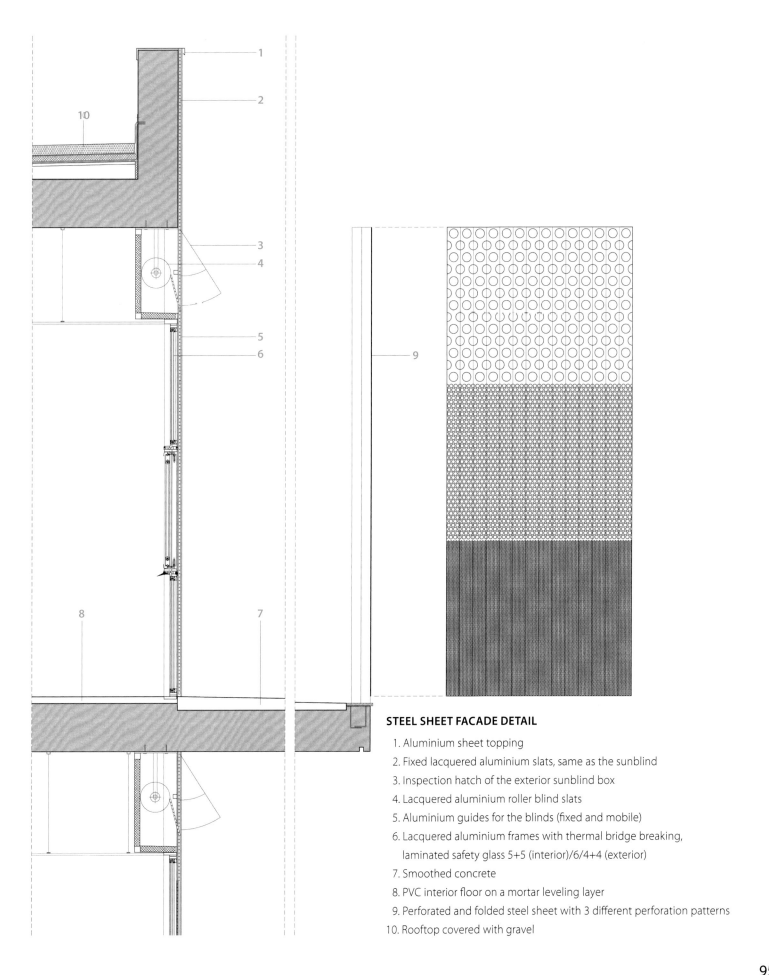

STEEL SHEET FACADE DETAIL

1. Aluminium sheet topping
2. Fixed lacquered aluminium slats, same as the sunblind
3. Inspection hatch of the exterior sunblind box
4. Lacquered aluminium roller blind slats
5. Aluminium guides for the blinds (fixed and mobile)
6. Lacquered aluminium frames with thermal bridge breaking, laminated safety glass 5+5 (interior)/6/4+4 (exterior)
7. Smoothed concrete
8. PVC interior floor on a mortar leveling layer
9. Perforated and folded steel sheet with 3 different perforation patterns
10. Rooftop covered with gravel

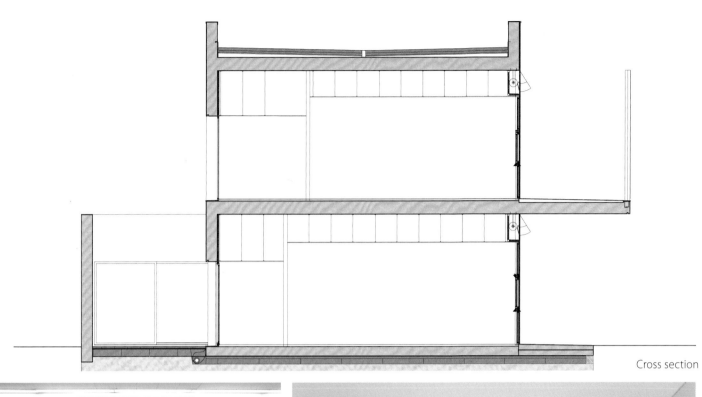

Cross section

Hirotani Yoshihiro + Ishida Yusaku / Archivision Hirotani Studio

Leimondo Nursery School

Nagahama, Shiga, Japan   **Photographs:** KurumataTamotsu and Archivision Hirotani Studio

This daycare for children aged zero to five years stands on the outskirts of Nagahama city in Shiga prefecture. The school has been planned as a single-storey structure with a feeling of transparency between each of the spaces as well as the exterior landscape and, the "House of Light", as we call it, has been placed in the main nursery area.

The features which give the project its name "House of Light" are conical, square light-wells of different shapes, different colors and facing different directions in the high ceiling bringing in various "lights" into the interior space, changing with the time and the seasons.

The children may be able to feel the changes of these "lights", even chase them and play with them, and to enjoy this gift of "light" in their daily activities. In this way, the project not only transforms something entirely natural into a game, surely the most sustainable of play, it also creates an awareness in the children from a young age of the changing of the seasons, as manifested in their everyday lives.

Furthermore, the shape of the "House of Light" may be seen from the outside as its unique silhouettes are outlined against the almost unchanging rural scenery, providing it with a little more character. Yet if the exterior of the house of light is curiously austere, if eccentric, in design, the interior is flooded with tranquil colorful light. Rooms are white, pink, yellow or green, and childrens furniture, tables and chairs in unfussy light wood, can be glimpsed through wall cut-outs, some shaped like windows, others like houses. Ceilings are uniformly high, but do not overwhelm the small occupants due to the bright, natural light that illuminates them. The different colors of the rooms creates distinct spaces while the similarities--the high ceilings, the cutouts, the uniformity of design--provide visual continuity. There is an overwhelming calm and dignity to both the outside and inside of the building.

Architecture:
Hirotani Yoshihiro + Ishida Yusaku /
Archivision Hirotani Studio
Art director:
Hirai Toru / Mars Design Workshop
Furniture design:
Koizumi Makoto
Structural engineering:
Umezawa structural engineers
Mechanical engineering:
Azuplanning
Client:
Social Welfare Corporation Lemonkai
Total area:
5,600 sqm (60,300 sqft)
Built area:
700 sqm (7,500 sqft)

1. Entrance	7. Nursery for age 4	13. House of light 5	19. Storage	25. Baby bathing room
2. Office	8. Nursery for age 5	14. House of light 6	20. Wind break room	26. Porch
3. Nursery for babies	9. House of light 1	15. House of light 7	21. Conference room	27. Play ground
4. Nursery for age 1	10. House of light 2	16. House of light 8	22. Dressing room	28. Parking lot
5. Nursery for age 2	11. House of light 3	17. House of light 9	23. Kitchen	
6. Nursery for age 3	12. House of light 4	18. Formular room	24. Multi-purpose room	

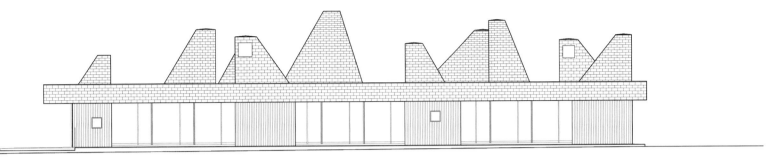

South elevation

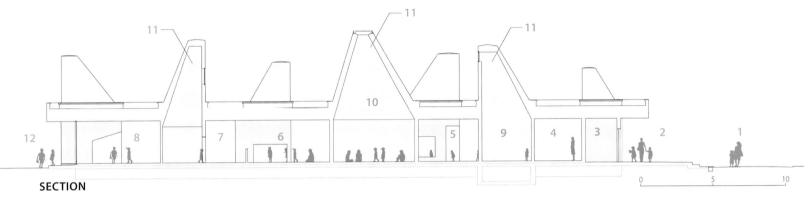

SECTION

1. Road
2. Porch
3. Entrance
4. Nursery for babies
5. Nursery for 1 yr olds
6. Nursery for 3 yr olds
7. Nursery for 4 yr olds
8. Nursery for 5 yr olds
9. Baby bathing room
10. Multi-purpose room
11. House of light (hol)
12. Playground

The school has been planned as a single-storey structure with a feeling of transparency between each of the spaces as well as the exterior landscape and, the "House of Light", as it is called, has been placed in the main nursery area.

103

The shape of the "House of Light" may be seen from the outside as its unique silhouettes are outlined against the almost unchanging rural scenery, providing it with a little more character. The different colors of the rooms creates distinct spaces while the similarities--the high ceilings, the cutouts, the uniformity of design--provide visual continuity.

SOLID architecture ZT GmbH

Kindergarten Neufeld an der Leitha

Neufeld an der Leitha, Burgenland, Austria

Photographs: Kurt Kuball

The design by SOLID architecture for the new, four group (two of them for nurseries) kindergarten, in Neufeld an der Leitha emerged as the winning project in an invited competition that sought designs for a new building to house a four-group kindergarten. One requirement of the competition was that it should be possible to add a further two groups without disrupting day-to-day activities at the kindergarten.

Placing the building volume in an east-west direction created clearly defined outdoor areas. Towards the north the building remains closed, and it is here that the vehicular approach, the car-parking area and the entrance are located. As a result the outdoor spaces in the south and west, which are reserved exclusively for the children, are largely undisturbed by traffic.

The interplay of daylight and architecture is an essential element of the design. In the interior the service zones and ancillary rooms face north. An open communicative central area flows through the entire building. Towards the south the rooms for the groups detach themselves from the building with large areas of glazing that allow the best possible use of daylight. Incisions made in the roof together with the outdoor areas allotted to the groups form new spaces with both indoor and outdoor characteristics. Staggering the units in a north-south direction establishes visual connections between the group rooms. The open spaces ascribed to the groups can be integrated into educational activities. They are a manageable size and break down the boundaries between inside and the constantly changing outdoor area.

Together with its sanitary facilities and storage space each of the group rooms forms an independent unit. Glass walls, skylights and the way the garden interlocks with the kindergarten create spaces flooded with daylight and different moods and colors.

The group rooms are open-design. Clearly defined play areas, such as a building corner or dolls' corner, were deliberately left out so as to allow the free combination of different play and work areas. Encounters in and withdrawal from the group are both possible. All areas are also accessible to children with physical disabilities. The dining room is positioned near the entrance and can also be used as a "parents' café". Skylights in the large roof extending over the entire building provide light for the central zone and the sanitary facilities. In the south the roof extends into a pergola with wooden slats. This helps protect the south-facing group rooms against overheating. Together with the wooden deck below it the pergola defines a sheltered transitional zone to the garden.

The building services concept focuses on an economic use of resources and protection of the environment. The entire building has a controlled ventilation system. The fresh air introduced via a subterranean tunnel is pre-warmed in winter and cooled in summer. Hot water is produced by means of a water-water heat pump. Rainwater seeps off into cisterns in the school grounds.

Architecture:

SOLID architecture ZT GmbH

Project Management:

Arch. DI Christine Horner

Collaborators:

Arch. DI Christoph Hinterreitner,
Arch. DI Tibor Tarcsay, DI Kristina Zaunschirm

Client:

Stadtgemeinde Neufeld an der Leitha

Structural Engineering :

RWT PLUS ZT GmbH;

Construction supervision:

BMG;

**Heat / Ventilation and
Electrical Engineering:**

HTB-PLAN Haustechnik Planungs GmbH

Built Area:

1,200 sqm (13,000 sqft)

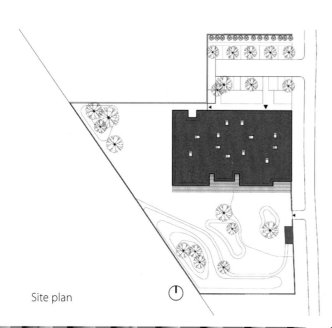

Site plan

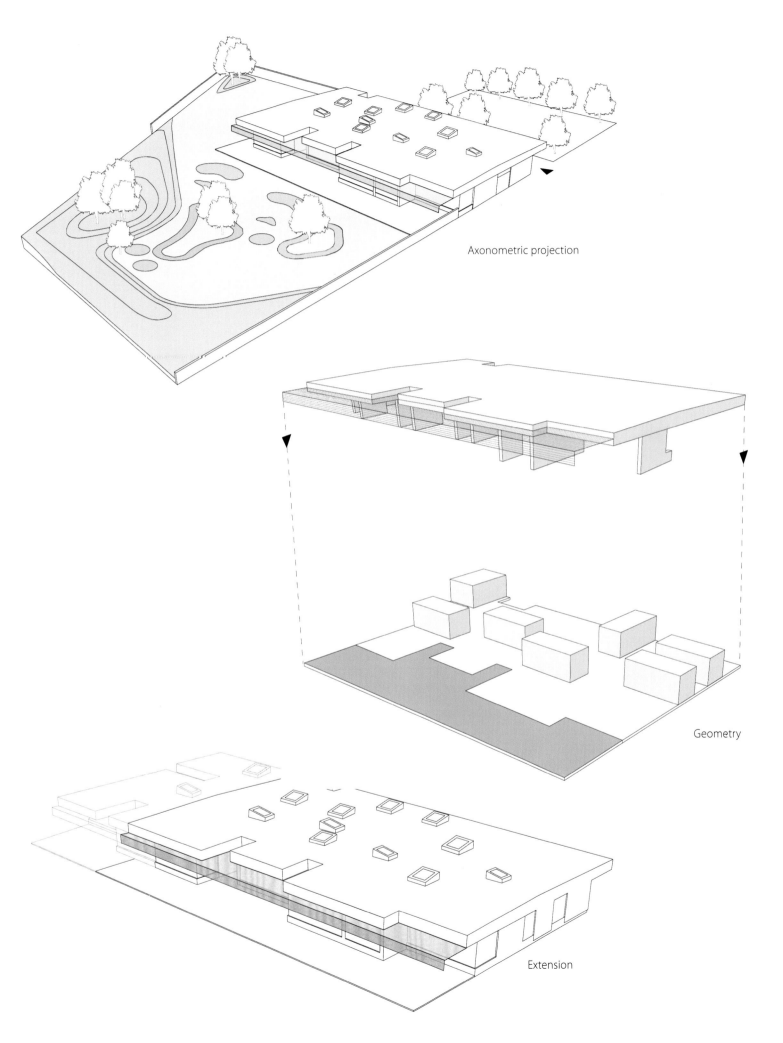

Axonometric projection

Geometry

Extension

111

Ground floor plan

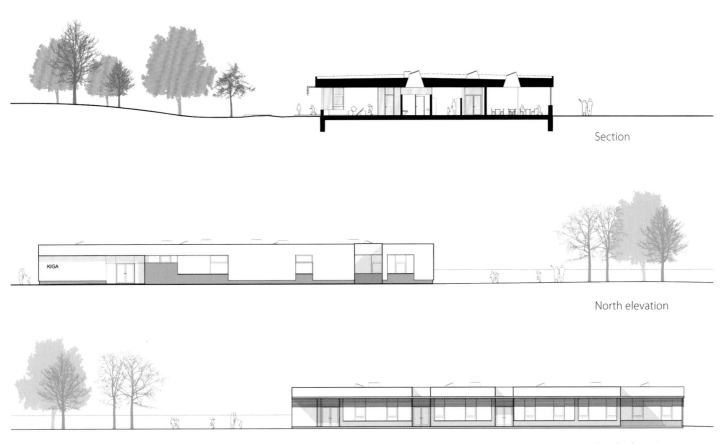

Section

North elevation

South elevation

The building services concept focuses on an economic use of resources and protection of the environment. The entire building has a controlled ventilation system.

All areas are also accessible to children with physical disabilities. The dining room is positioned near the entrance and can also be used as a "parents' café". Skylights in the large roof extending over the entire building provide light for the central zone and the sanitary facilities.

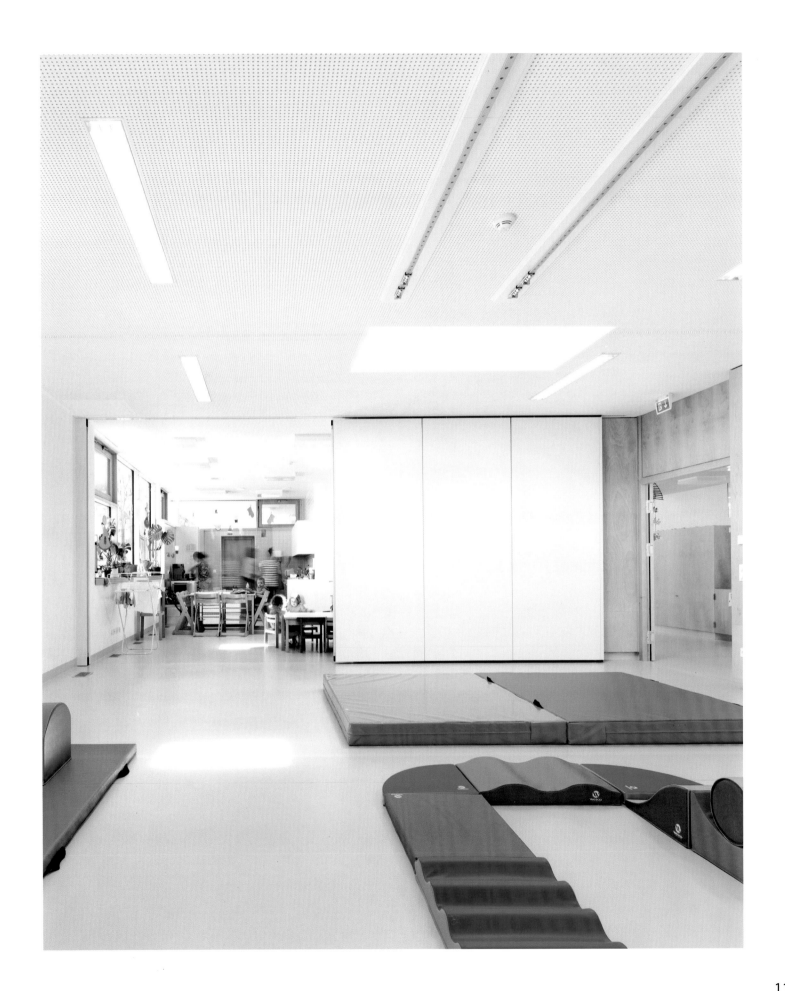

Dorte Mandrup Arkitekter ApS

Skanderborggade Day Care Center

Copenhagen, Denmark

Photographs: Jens Markus Lindhe

The client wanted a three-unit day care institution/nursery school, with the potential to be converted into kindergarten units, composed of three rooms for three respective day care/nursery groups, each with an accompanying changing room, a common room, cloakroom, kitchen, administration and secondary rooms.

The district zoning plan provides for institutional buildings of no more than one story. In order to fulfill the client's requirement for an outdoor area equal to that of the built area, it was thus a prerequisite that the outdoor areas had to emplaced on the roof.

The ground level floor surface folds upwards to form a hill or slope that connects the ground and roof. The slope is furnished with large outdoor sack chairs designed specifically for this purpose. The sack chairs ensure safe play on the ramp, while parasols can be fixed in the middle of the sack chairs to provide shade if needed. The ramp serves as a seating area when there are events. Underneath the slope is an unheated space where a forest of columns is used for swings and other forms of play, when the weather is cold or wet. Two other light wells cut into the roof plane ensure daylight and a variety of outdoor spaces in conjunction with the other rooms of the building.

The slope connects directly with a flat roof garden, which is enclosed by a white semi-transparent polyester fabric that allows for the maximum amount of openness and light intake. The garden is arranged through a series of colored circles and mounds which allow for a variety of facilities, such as a barbeque area, sandboxes, water zone, etc. The rest of the roof surface can be used more freely, for example as a roadway for moon cars and tricycles.

Other outdoor areas include a courtyard in the northwestern corner, with a scale that creates the perfect environment for more concentrated, quieter play, and the napping area courtyard, which is planted with tall standard deciduous trees that filter the summer sun through their leaves. This area gives access to the day care institution's napping area, which has been placed in a corner that is protected from street noise.

Architecture:
Dorte Mandrup Arkitekter ApS
Engineer:
Jørn Tækker A/S
Contractor:
NCC Brøndby
Client:
City of Copenhagen,
Department of Labor & Family Affairs
Outdoor play area:
490 sqm (5,274 sqft)

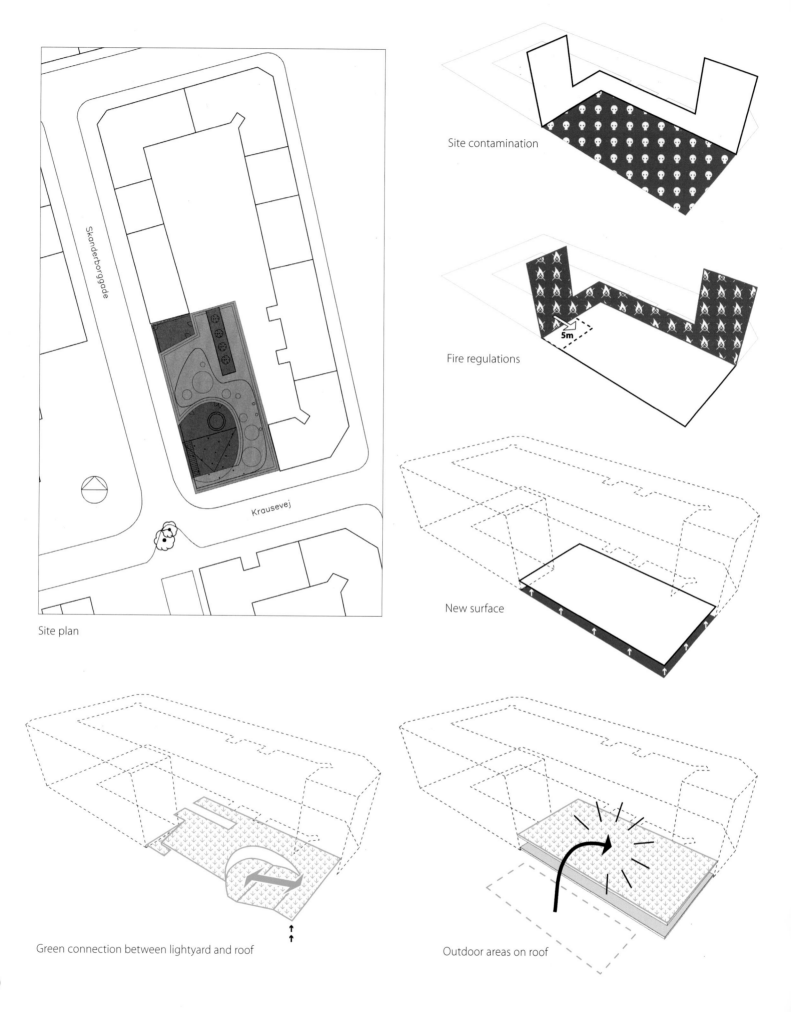

Site plan

Site contamination

Fire regulations

New surface

Green connection between lightyard and roof

Outdoor areas on roof

120

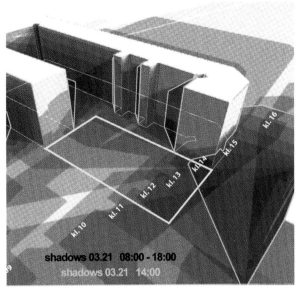

Sun orientation

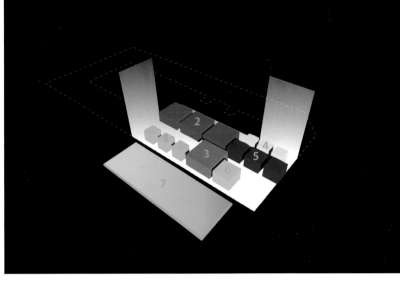

PROGRAMME

1. Nursing area 3x9 m²
2. Group rooms 3x45 m²
3. Common area 50 m²
4. Staff rooms 3x8 m²
5. Cloakroom 3x15 m²
6. Kitchen 20 m²
7. Outdoor area 300 m²

Shaping of surface according to light, air and regulations

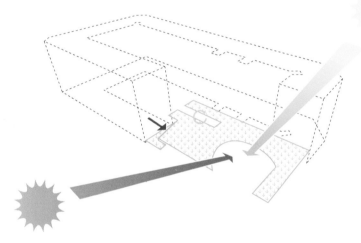

Zoning regulations due to sunlight

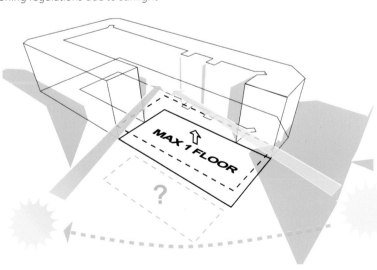

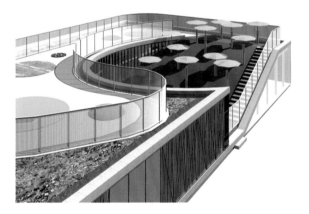

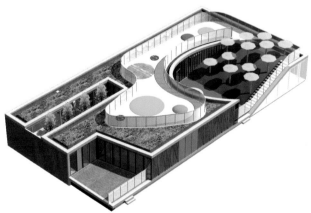

The roof garden slope and courtyard are surfaced with red granulated rubber. The flat area is scattered with hills and mounds made from the same material in green, blue and yellow, while on the slope are outdoor sack chairs upholstered in tarpaulin cloth and fixed in place with galvanized steel mounts, and with built-in parasol bases.

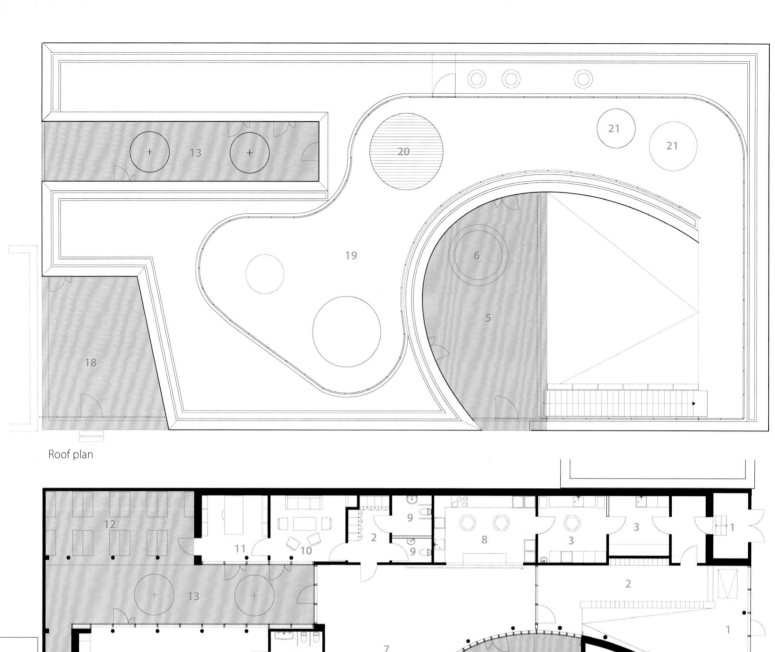

Roof plan

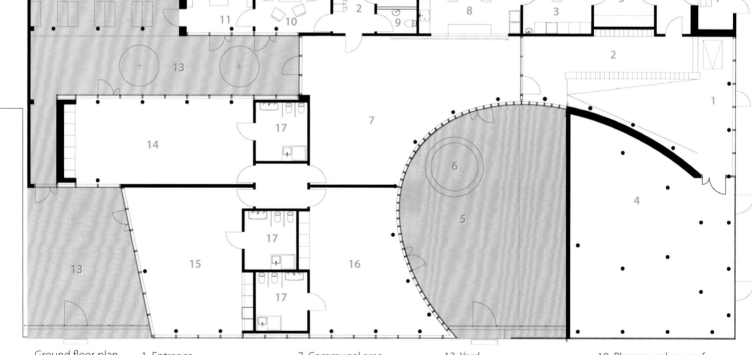

Ground floor plan

1. Entrance	7. Communal area	13. Yard	19. Playground on roof
2. Cloakroom	8. Kitchen	14. Nurserybay 1	20. Wood
3. Utility room	9. Restroom	15- Nurserybay 2	21. Slope
4. Playground with swings	10. Meeting room	16. Nurserybay 3	
5. Playground	11. Office	17. Diaper changing facility	
6. Sand box	12. Open-air shelter	18. Yard grass	

The area underneath the slope is a subsidiary space used as an unheated play zone. The space is screened to the south and west by polycarbonate, which takes advantage of passive solar heating during the winter months.

Other outdoor areas include a courtyard in the northwestern corner, with a scale that creates the perfect environment for more concentrated, quieter play, and the napping area courtyard, which is planted with tall standard deciduous trees that filter the summer sun through their leaves. This area gives access to the day care institution's napping area.

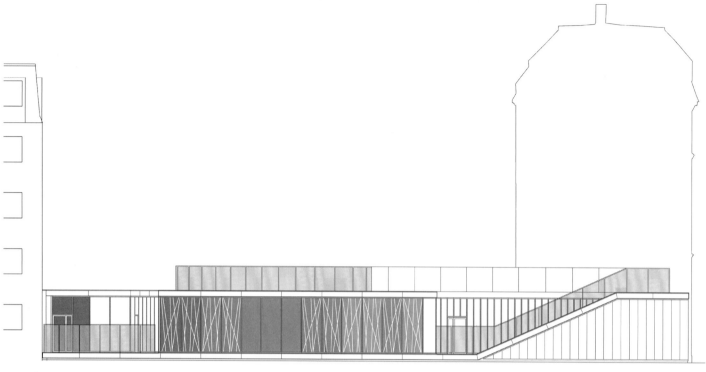

West façade

126

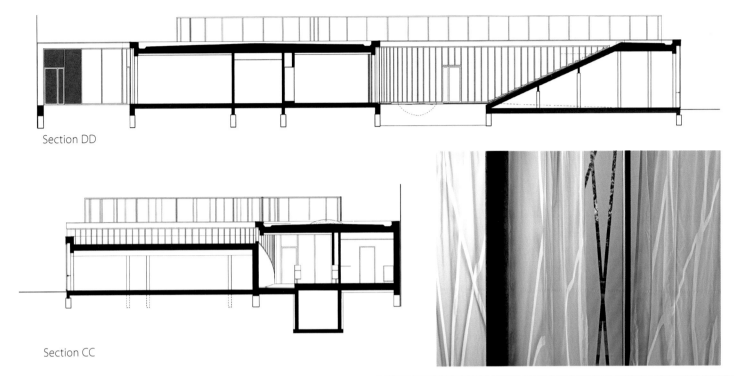

Section DD

Section CC

Paul Le Quernec & Michel Grasso

La Bulle Enchantée

Sarreguemines, France

Photographs: Guillaume Duret, Michel Grasso and Paul le Quernec

The project is designed as a body cell, placing the nursery at the center of the layout as the nucleus, the surrounding gardens as the cytoplasm, and a circumscribing enclosing wall as the membrane. A large outdoor playground is created through a continuous curvilinear wall that shapes out the boundaries of the facility. The "vaginal" entrance is characterized by a concrete vault, which is a continuation of the peripheral wall. Floating within its membrane, the nursery welcomes visitors into a round space at the center of the building, with a covered patio. All the children's areas radiate outwards from this central room. This concept of transitional space and centripetal walkway avoids all corridor effects, and there is no break in the movement; the playrooms spread out like a hand-held fan ideally oriented southward, each one terminating in its own playground. The curved lines of the walls and ceilings underline the organic and womb-like concept, providing safety and comfort within the building for children and parents alike.

The ceiling height in the surrounding playrooms is 2.10 meters (6.9 ft) high so as to create a comfortable environment for the babies and children. Highlighting this idea, we combined it with a variation of ceiling heights of up to 4.2 meters (13.8 ft), creating a large range of spaces and volumes. Thanks to this contrasting effect, the units with low ceilings are perceived as protective recesses, and are more dimly lit than the areas with higher ceilings, which have zenithal light. This creates greater contrast between the various uses of areas of the building, but the transition between different ceiling heights occurs smoothly due to the curving walls, which also generate reflective light on the ceilings.

Considering the children's perception of the building, it was decided to turn it into a row of variously dimensioned boxes, growing out of a bush of bamboo, capturing the daylight. This idea not only has an aesthetic function, but the bamboo also provides shade and prevents the building from overheating while the hat shaped boxes regulate the energy intake depending on the season.

Architecture:
Paul le Quernec, representative architect ;
Michel Grasso, associate

Project team:
BET Jost (heating and ventilation
system engineer),
HN ingénierie (structural engineer),
E3 économie (building costs consultant),
François Liermann (sustainability consultant),
Ingemansson (acoustic consultant),
Ecotral (restauration consultant)

Client:
Communauté d'Agglomération
Sarreguemines Confluences

Capacity:
55 to 60 children

Floor area:
1,400 sqm (15,100 sqft)

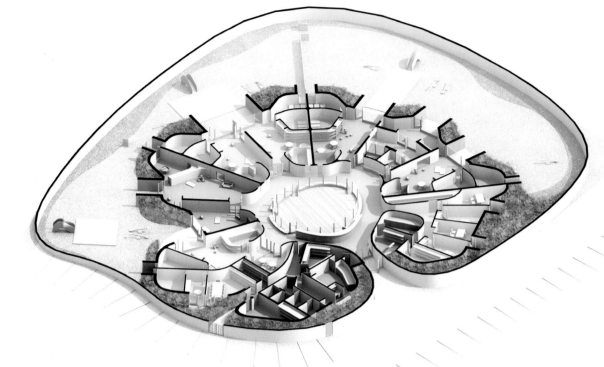

Axonometric projection

Sections

Elevations

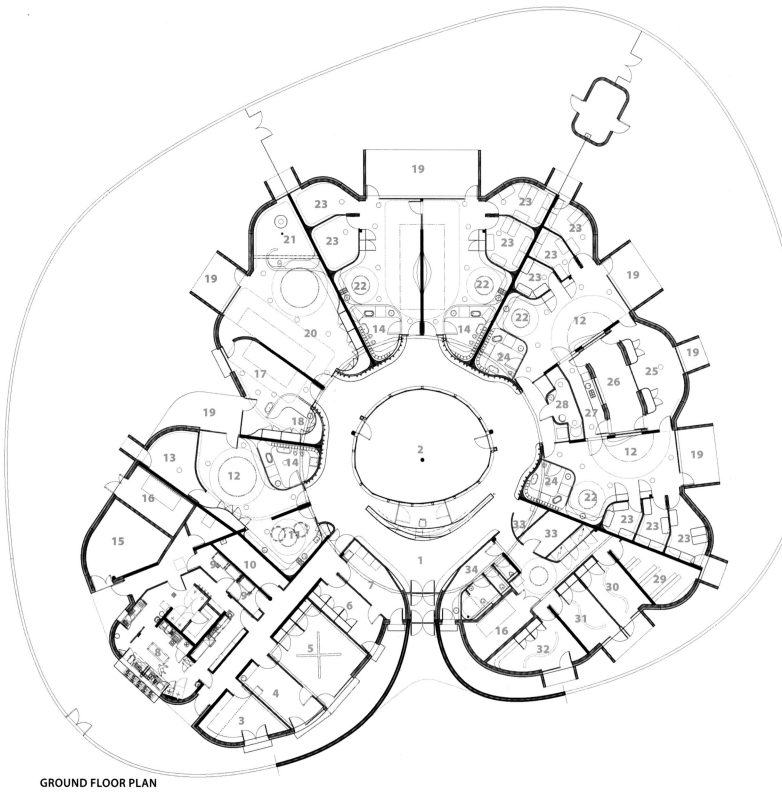

GROUND FLOOR PLAN

1. Entrance, reception area
2. Covered exterior space
3. Women´s dressing rooms
4. Tearoom
5. Meeting rooms
6. Laundry storeroom
7. Laundry
8. Kitchen
9. Garbage area
10. Cleaning area
11. Teachers´ kitchen
12. Free play space
13. Rest area
14. Washrooms
15. Boiler
16. Air treatment systems
17. Education activities
18. Wardrobes
19. Terraces
20. Psychomotor
21. Showers
22. Eating area
23. Sleeping area
24. Changing area
25. Babies´ psychomotor
26. Patio
27. Bottle room
28. Lactation room
29. Archives
30. Men´s dressing rooms
31. Office
32. Management office
33. Storeroom
34. Staff washroom

Emplacement

Considering the children's perception of the building, we decided to turn it into a row of variously dimensioned boxes, growing out of a bush of bamboo, capturing the day light. This idea not only has an aesthetical function; the bamboo will also provide shade that will prevent the building from overheating while the hat shaped boxes regulate the energy intake depending on season.

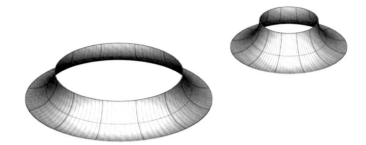

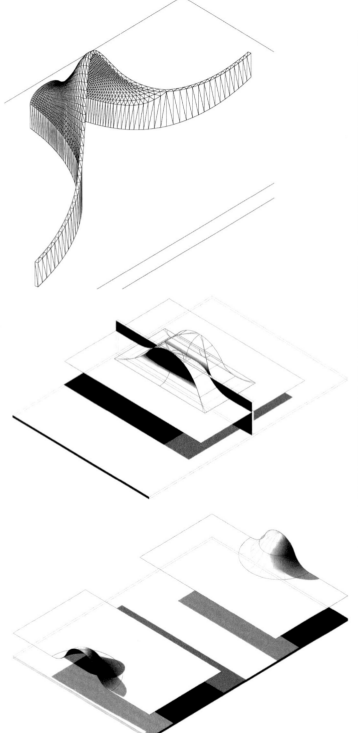

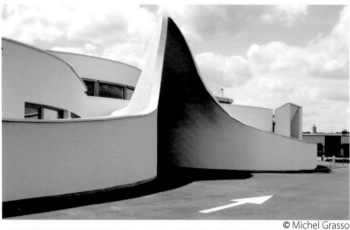

© Michel Grasso

© Paul le Quernec

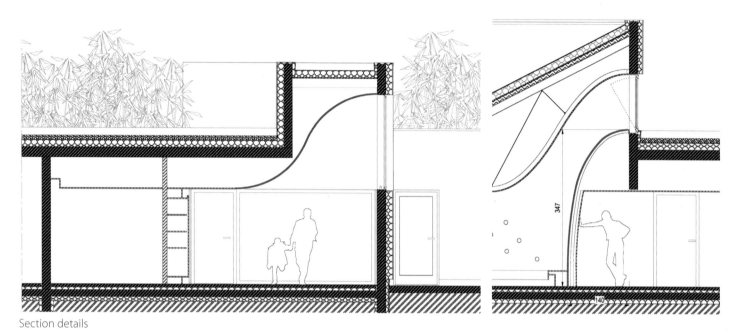

Section details

© Michel Grasso

© Michel Grasso

© Paul le Quernec

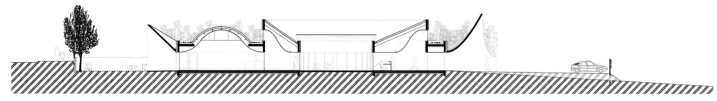

Cross section

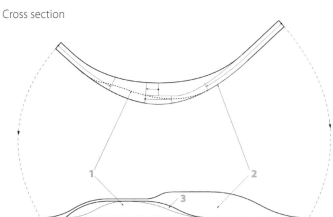

© Paul le Quernec

© Paul le Quernec

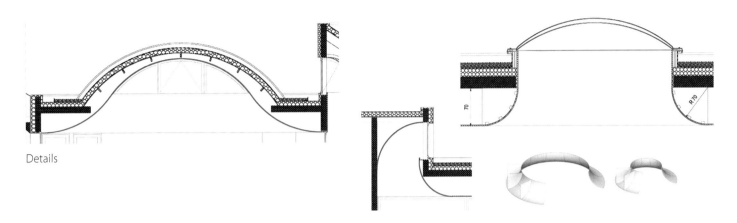

Details

© Paul le Quernec

© Paul le Quernec

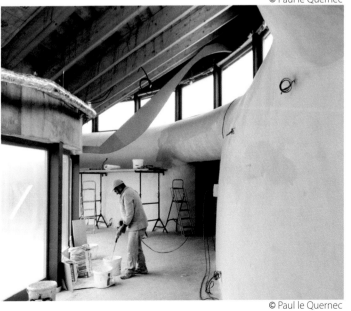

© Paul le Quernec

JKMM Architects

House of Children in Saunalahti

Espoo, Finland

Photographs: Mika Huisman, Robert Lindström, Päivi Meuronen

The motto of this competition entry for a day-care/nursery in Saunalahti in the City of Espoo was "Mato Matala" ("The Lowly Worm," by Richard Scarry). In addition to being a childcare center, the house also functions as a common space for inhabitants of the local area.

The rendered, curved south wall forms the building's public façade. The other façades are of timber and they open towards the sloping, pine-covered hill. The building is located at a difficult, rocky site approximately 1 km from seashore. In order to maintain a large area for the playground within the yard and to create sound barrier against the noise of traffic, the building adapts the dimensions of the yard against the edge of the cliff on the border of the site. It has been demanding job to make the lot and playground unobstructed, safe and exhilarating for the children within the available budget of the project.

The first floor will house the day-care centre with three units containing five groups and common spaces. The home areas open out on the yard that is formed between the rising hill slope behind and the new building. The street side contains common and staff facilities, while the ground floor contains the children's nursery and technical spaces.

The main structure of the building is made out of concrete. The southwest façade is light masonry with joint sealing. Other façades are plastered, with wooden frame windows. Skylight windows open down to the entry hall of each unit. The main materials on the outside are white masonry, light plaster, aluminium and pine - inside ash floors on playrooms, plastered wall surfaces and filler floorings in the lobbies, green tufted carpet on the walls and ceilings of the corridors and downstairs lobby and light acoustic paper-coating on the ceilings.

Special light fittings, fixtures and some of other furniture have been specially designed for this building. The design of the building is intended to stimulate children with images of a fairy-tale world.

Architecture:
JKMM Architects, Samuli Miettinen, Asmo Jaaksi, Teemu Kurkela, Juha Mäki-Jyllilä

Project team, additional members:
Katja Savolainen, project architect;
Christopher Delaney, project architect during construction phase;
Päivi Meuronen, interior architect;
Edit Bajsz, Aaro Martikainen, Ilona Palmunen, Merita Soini

Client:
City of Espoo
Lars Hagman, city architect
Pirjo Sundholm, project manager
Katja Peltola-Metsälä, project manager during construction phase
Juha Hovinen constructor architect

Site area:
5,500 sqm (59,200)

Built area:
1,800 sqm (19,400)

à Huisman

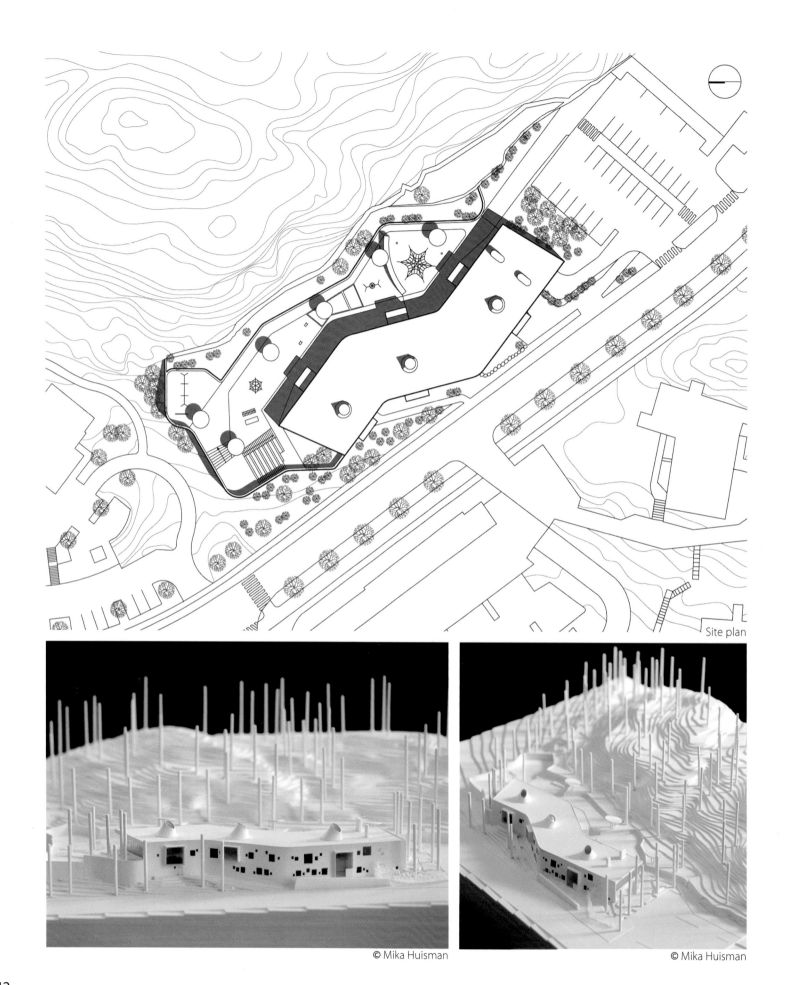

Site plan

© Mika Huisman

© Mika Huisman

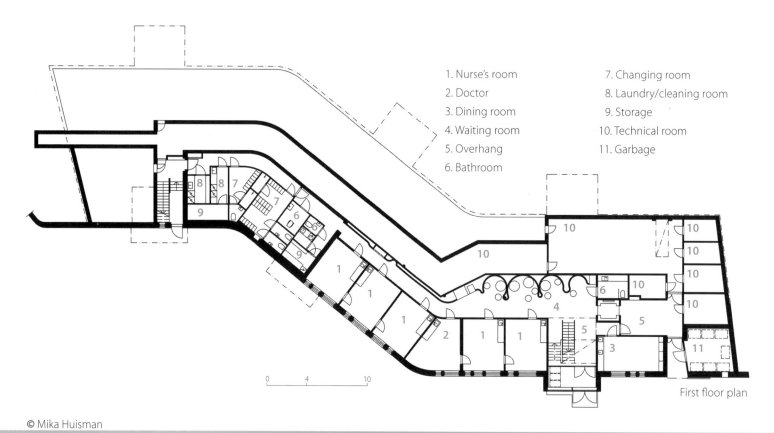

1. Nurse's room
2. Doctor
3. Dining room
4. Waiting room
5. Overhang
6. Bathroom
7. Changing room
8. Laundry/cleaning room
9. Storage
10. Technical room
11. Garbage

First floor plan

© Mika Huisman

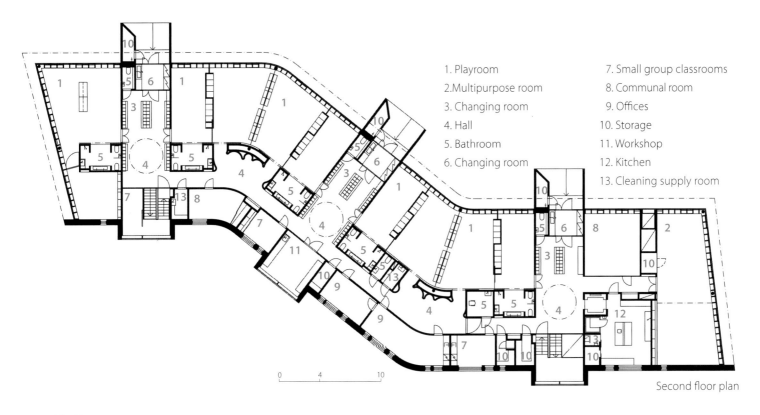

1. Playroom
2. Multipurpose room
3. Changing room
4. Hall
5. Bathroom
6. Changing room
7. Small group classrooms
8. Communal room
9. Offices
10. Storage
11. Workshop
12. Kitchen
13. Cleaning supply room

0   4   10

Second floor plan

© Mika Huisman

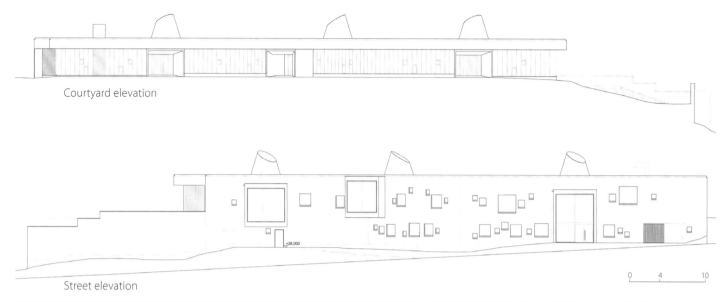

Courtyard elevation

Street elevation

+26.000

0 4 10

© Mika Huisman

© Mika Huisman

Special light fittings, fixtures and some of other furniture have been specially designed for this building. The design of the building is intended to stimulate children with images of a fairy-tale world.

© Mika Huisman

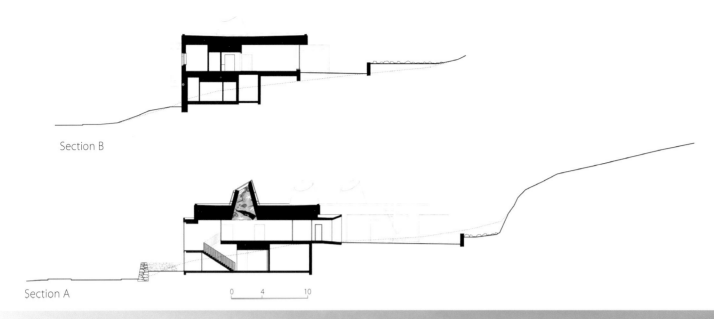

Section B

Section A

0   4   10

© Mika Huisman

© Mika Huisman

© Mika Huisman

The motto of this competition entry for a day-care/nursery in Saunalahti in the City of Espoo was "Mato Matala" ("The Lowly Worm," by Richard Scarry. In addition to being a childcare center, the house also functions as a common space for inhabitants of the local area.

© Mika Huisman

150

© Mika Huisman

© Robert Lindström

© Mika Huisman

© Robert Lindström

Taller Sau & Lluís Jordà Sala

La Cabanya Nursery

Torelló, Spain

Photographs: Adrià Goula

The nursery is both a part of and separate from the park of the same name that houses it. At a slightly higher elevation than the rest of the park, the location takes full advantage of its location and the views afforded.

The school comprises of three buildings in a triangular arrangement, joined by a skylit courtyard in the center, which links the other spaces of the program together, serves as an extension of the dining area, as a performance hall, as a patio.

The program consists of three intertwined parts: classroom space, management, and services, with the entrance on the north edge and a vertical circulation edge parallel to the main road to the east. A series of ramps serve the second floor and provide additional access from the street. They also give the school a striking appearance, with the floating roof and a wide expanse of glass that affords passers-by a glance into the triangular core.

On the North edge entrance, there is a top-floor cantilever extending towards the small courtyard, drawing the eye to the main entrance and presenting a colorful face.

Overhead a series of south-facing, solar-paneled skylights, in addition to clerestories, provide plenty of natural light. The classrooms face south and are separated from the courtyard by a transparent façade covered with interactive panels that regulate the amount of light that comes in, providing a secondary purpose as a game for the children. The classrooms share use of some outdoor rooms covered by glazed canopies for sun protection. Beyond these is the courtyard, and behind the brightly colored exterior wall is space for a Nap Room. The space under the ramps is used for storing strollers.

The entrance is wood-paneled, while the classrooms' façade is raw concrete. The vertical connections are separated by glass façade printed with a drawing of the Torelló landscape.

Architecture:
Taller Sau and Lluís Jordà Sala
Client:
Torelló Townhall
Area:
1,000 sqm (10,800 sqft)

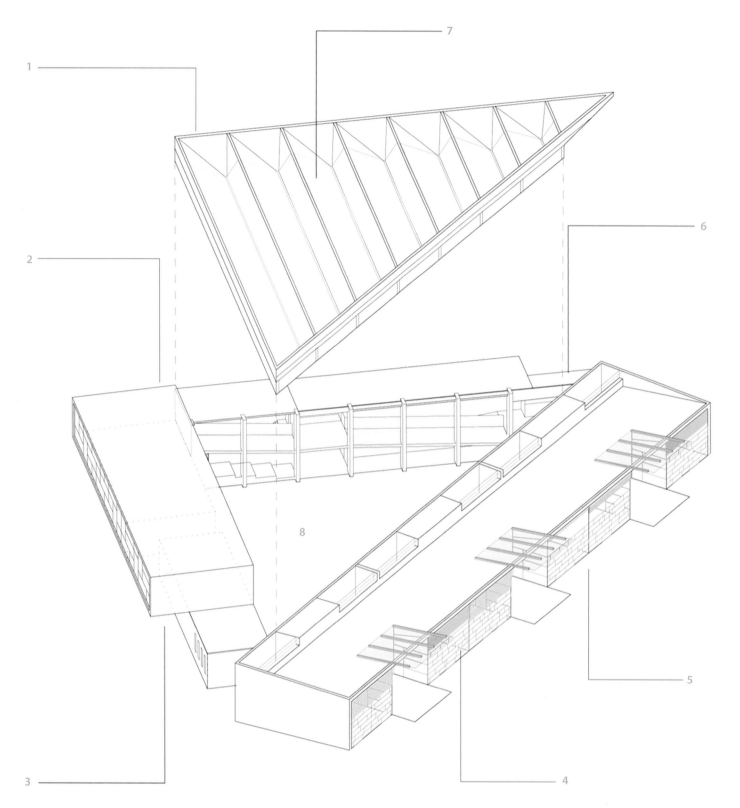

1. Roof: Protects the inner courtyard of the nursery. Wooden structure, translucent glass and diaphanous space create the feeling of being outside. The inclined planes to the south are covered by solr panels.

2. Teacher module: Located at the top. Visually related to the interior and exterior courtyards. Generantes the entrance cantilever.

3. Dining roomand service module: Between the entry courtyard and the inner courtyard we find the modules that contain the kitchen and dining facilities that when openend can invade the inner courtyard.

4. Interactive panels: the glazed façade is divided into regulate the entry of light and can be used as a game.

5. Classrooms module: Contains all the clasrooms of the nursery. Each classroom shares a porch that brings us to the more private outsoor patio.

6. Connector module: Connect the diferent levels through ramps. We use the space under ramps as a stroller parking.

7. Solar panels

8. Inner courtyard.

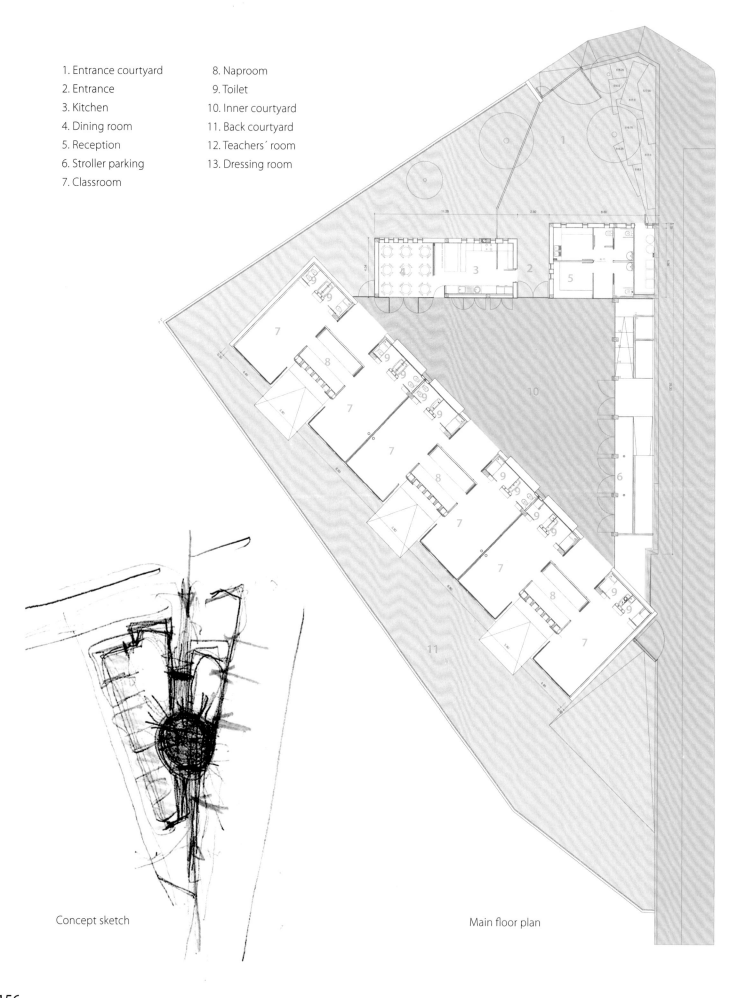

1. Entrance courtyard
2. Entrance
3. Kitchen
4. Dining room
5. Reception
6. Stroller parking
7. Classroom
8. Naproom
9. Toilet
10. Inner courtyard
11. Back courtyard
12. Teachers´ room
13. Dressing room

Concept sketch

Main floor plan

The school comprises of three buildings in a triangular arrangement, joined by a skylit space in the center, which links the other spaces of the program together, serves as an extension of the dining area, as a performance hall, as a patio.

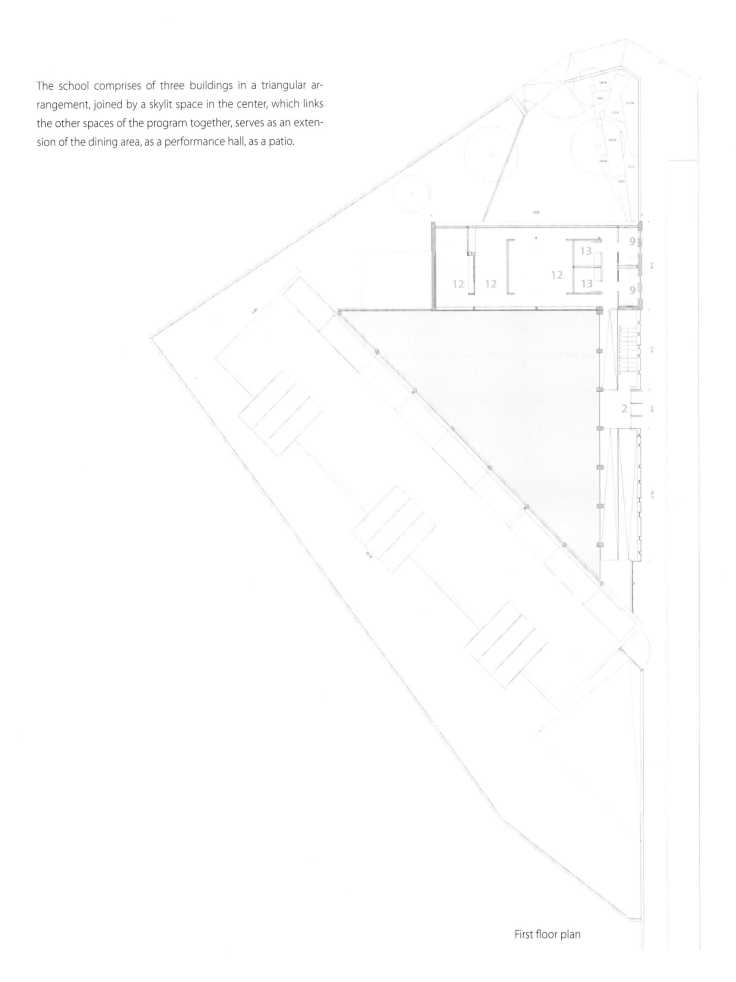

First floor plan

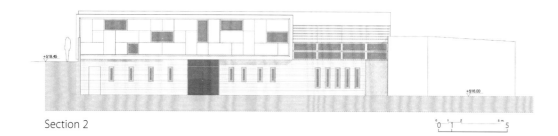

Section 2

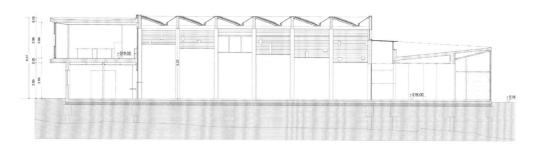

Section 3

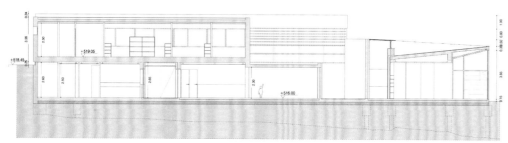

Section 5

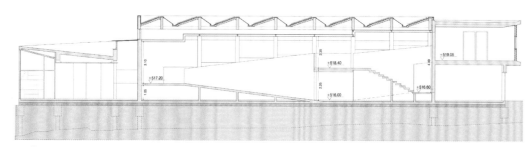

Section 6

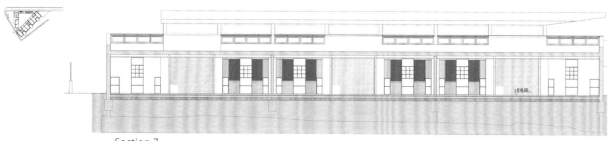

Section 7

159

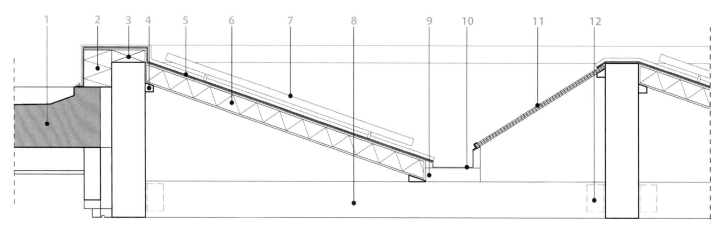

INNER COURTYARD ROOF CONSTRUCTION DETAIL

1. Deck slab
2. Isolation
3. Wooden profile 20x7 cm
4. Piece of wood 5x5 cm
5. Zinc plate
6. Insulating sandwich panel
7. Photovoltaic panel witn fasteners
8. Wooden belt
9. Wooden profile
10. Rainwater collector
11. Policarbonate panel 16 mm
12. T profile between belts

WALL DETAIL

1. Zinc plate
2. Metal bar
3. Wooden panel
4. Metallic sandwich panel with 7 cm isolation
5. Laminated wood girder
6. Interior drywall
7. Polystyrene isolation panel
8. Fenolic panel
9. metal profile
10. Wooden list
11. Vertical batten
12. Aluminium frames
13. Double laminated glass
14. Foam PVC flooring
15. Pipes for underfloor heating
16. Suport with dividers for tubes
17. Concrete slab
18. Gravel layer

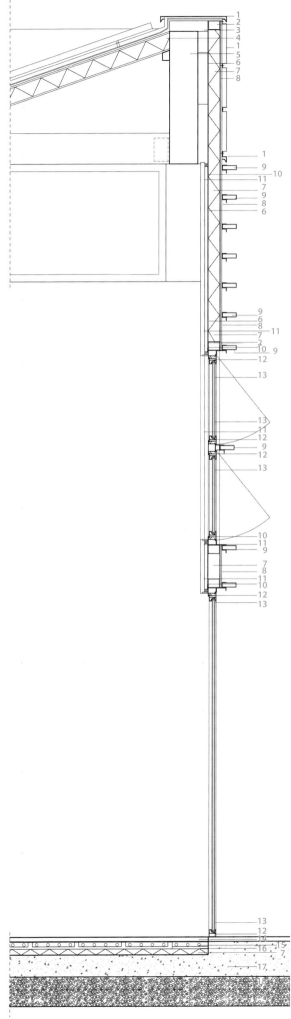

v-architekten

The Blue Nursery

Monheim am Rhein, Germany

Photographs: Constantin Meyer

The town of Monheim am Rhein is currently undergoing a number of significant changes. The local government hopes to ignite a successful city plan through a series of urban and social projects. The construction of the "Blue Nursery" is part of the change for this grey, outlying area. Each of the five units is conceived as its own separate "house."

The different degrees at which the roof slopes accentuates each of the houses while at the same time bringing everything together into a coherent whole characterized by the striking use of the color blue. Instead of corridors, intermediate play areas have been created at the entrance to each classroom. All of the main spaces are oriented towards the garden, which is on the south side of the lot.

Due to budgetary restrictions and the limited time available, a clear structure was chosen with an economic façade. The interior is made up of bearing concrete walls surrounded by a system of wooden frames. The final layer of the façade is a polyurethane dispersion that completely covers the building. Each group of children has been assigned a different color, which is the main color in their unit, and the support services associated with it. It is applied to the floors, walls and glazed tiles, and helps give each area a distinct character which is also popular with the children and encourages them to identify with their space.

Architecture:
v-architekten gmbh
(Tim Denninger, Jan Hertel,
Markus Kilian, Diana Reichle,
Michael Scholz)

Collaborators:
Marc Knechtges

Project Manager:
Stefan Nix-Pauleit, Architect

Structures:
S·G·B Spiessbach-Gerhards-Berg-GmbH

Landscaping:
Grünart

Technical Team:
HPI-Himmen Ingenieurgesellschaft

Client:
Monheim am Rhein City Hall

Built area:
900 sqm (9,700 sqft)

Site plan

Each of the five units is conceived as its own separate "house." The different degrees at which the roof slopes accentuates each of the houses while at the same time bringing everything together into a coherent whole characterized by the striking use of the color blue.

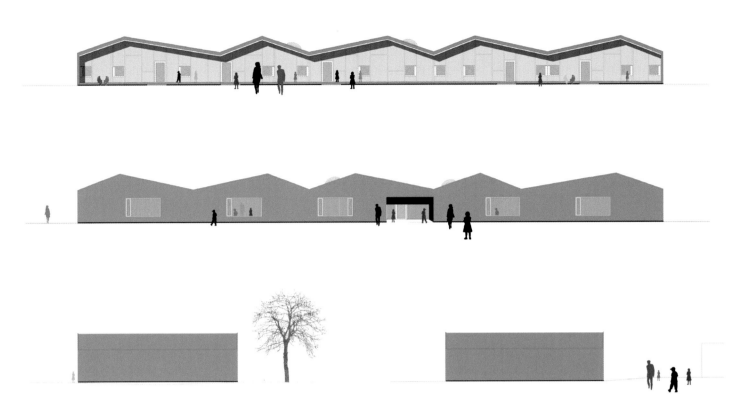

Elevations

FLOOR PLAN

1. Classroom
2. Classroom/Sleeping area
3. Gym
4. Play area
5. Office
6. Staff

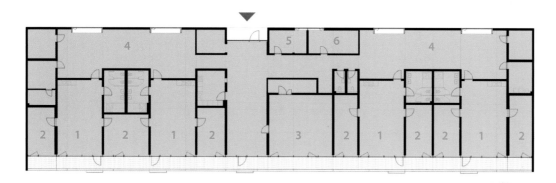

NEXT architects and Claudia Linders

Hestia Day-Care Centre

Rivierenbuurt, Amsterdam, The Netherlands

Photographs: Jeroen Musch

The Hestia Day-Care Centre follows the philosophy of Reggio Emilia, a philosophy that contains a number of explicit statements on architecture, which have been translated into a spatial concept for the new building.

The building is conceived as a city, as a collection of rooms, and it becomes a collection of different spaces in which the children can discover new places all the time in an exciting voyage of discovery. All of the spaces are connected to each other just as they are in a real city and the children can go from a big room to a small one, from a high room to a low one.

A framework of service modules provides structure: the various spaces are organized to fit into a grid. The main body includes all service modules, such as sanitary facilities, storerooms and bedrooms.

There is a strong sense of interior-exterior continuity: the grid is not confined to the building but also becomes the design concept for the exterior space. The rooms may be decorated with different hard surfaces and plants. The exterior, meanwhile, is extended throughout the building by designing various rooms like exterior space.

There are also different perceptions of scale, to engage the small inhabitants of the building. The different scales can be experienced as a result of the subtle use of height differences between the rooms themselves. In the central space, the large scale is perceptible because of the way the group spaces are separated, a smaller scale can be observed in the height differences height and an even smaller scale in the sheltered spaces.

Architecture:
NEXT architects and Claudia Linders

Team:
Marijn Schenk, Claudia Linders,
Bart Reuser and Michel Schreinemacher
with Joost Lemmens, Emanuelle Faustle,
Pieter Mulder, Filipe Pocas,
Daniel Aw and Marieke Spits

Structural Engineering:
Pieters Bouwtechniek

Mechanical engineering:
Valstar Simonis

Main contractor:
Reimert bouw en infrastructuur

Client:
Hestia

Floor area:
560 sqm (6,000 sqft)

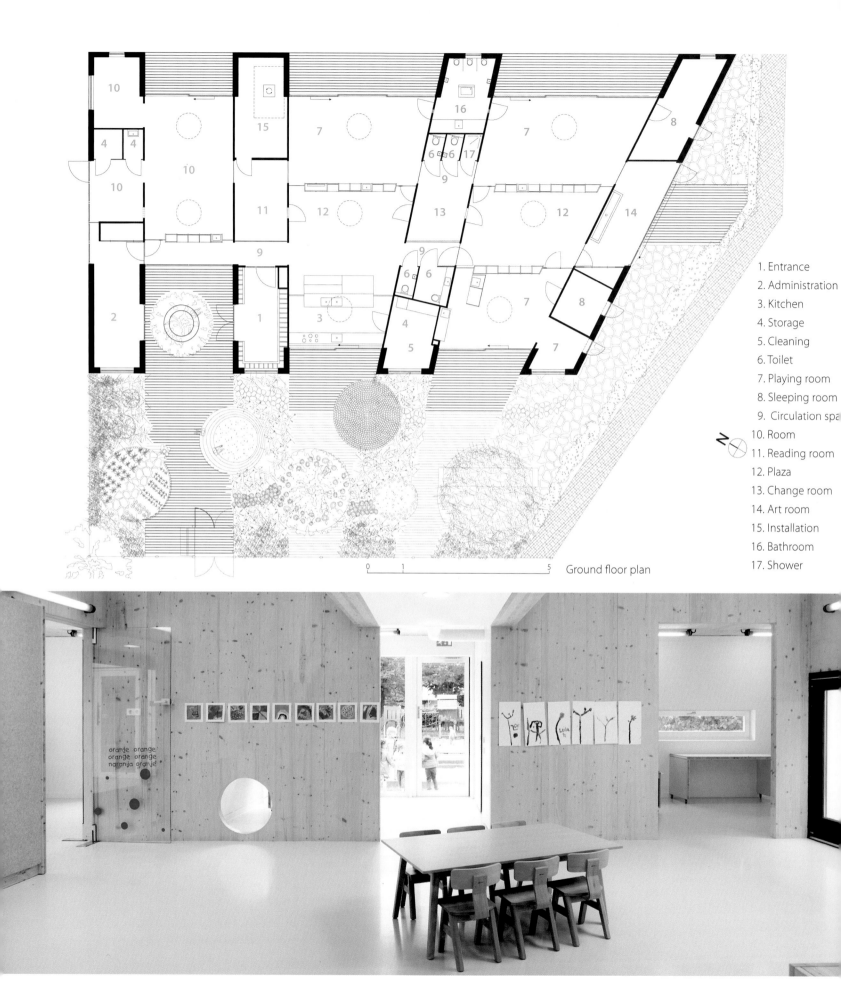

Ground floor plan

1. Entrance
2. Administration
3. Kitchen
4. Storage
5. Cleaning
6. Toilet
7. Playing room
8. Sleeping room
9. Circulation spa[...]
10. Room
11. Reading room
12. Plaza
13. Change room
14. Art room
15. Installation
16. Bathroom
17. Shower

0   1   5

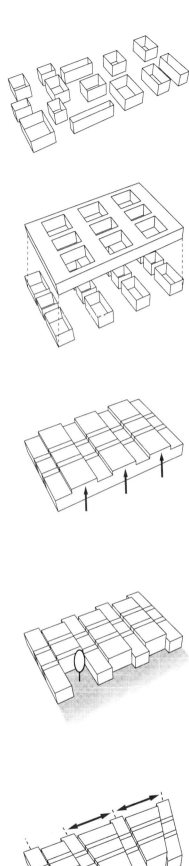

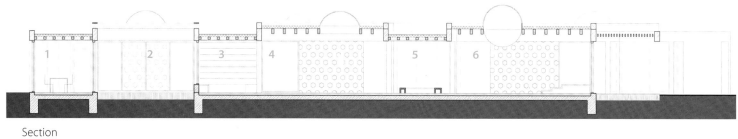

Section

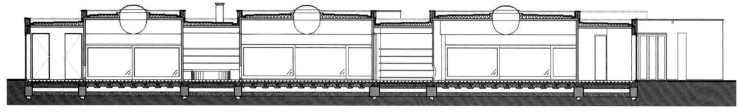

Section AA

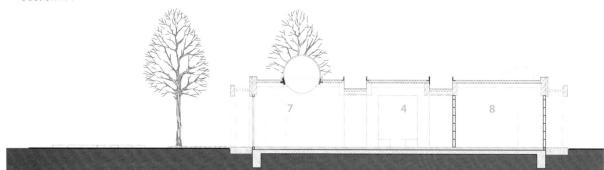

Section BB

1. Classroom
2. Patio
3. Library
4. Central courtyard
5. Changeroom
6. Theater
7. Kitchen
8. Playroom

There are also different perceptions of scale, to engage the small inhabitants of the building. The different scales can be experienced as a result of the subtle use of height differences between the rooms themselves.

Fluor Architects

Family Crèche in Drulingen

Drulingen, France   **Photographs:** Fluor Architects, contributed by agence volume2

Architecture:
Fluor Architects

The nursery is situated on a very small piece of land, which would seem at odds with the mission. Yet the project has risen poetically to the occasion to create a space where the children thrive and the staff work comfortably. The facility is seen as a cocoon sheltering those who are most fragile, it conjures up the idea of quiet protection, and rigor and cleanliness reign in this leisure space where the child starts his life in society.

The building is sheltered by a wooden shell--and envelope in both the physical and symbolic sense of the term. Like a skin protecting the nursery from the fast-paced world surrounding, the envelope is a border between everyday life and the warm and cozy family environment within the crèche.

The design of the crèche had to accommodate different uses: a flexible-attendance childcare center for up to 40 children, a drop-in center for parents and children, a child-minding facility, a daycare center for 30 children, and a kitchen capable of preparing 100 meals. The exteriors are included in the design, while the design of the drop-off spaces and surroundings were financed by the municipality. The site imposed constraints, being sparse and roughly triangular in shape, and already containing a police station (subsequently refurbished as offices and dwellings). The plot is located at the entrance to the town, bordering the local county road.

The concrete frame (in-situ concrete walls and hollow-core slabs) is externally insulated to give an important thermal inertia which helps maintain a steady interior temperature. Timber louvres on a timber frame are linked to the façade by galvanized steel profiles. On the street, the Siberian larch mesh and cladding of the envelope protects the external insulation, while the back is covered with a light-colored render. The flat roofs of the building are planted, with the exception of the yard on the first floor, which is covered with waterproof concrete screed and surrounded by a fence with an uneven pace. The window frames, in Siberian larch or in painted pine, were made by the carpenter in charge of the whole project.

On the inside, studs and suspended acoustic ceilings are all in plasterboard, and the floor heating system is covered with a rubber floor. The sanitary facilities were provided by Villeroy & Bosch, the plugs and switches are from the German brand Jung. The children's furniture has been selected from the Haba catalogue.

Located in Alsace in North-eastern France, the project consumes 140kWhep/sqm/year (for a contextualized target of 156kWhep/sqm/year) hence a gain of 10 % compared to the current Energy Consumption Guidelines. The building can be considered « HEP High environmental performance » (which wasn't a requirement and wasn't budgeted for by the client).

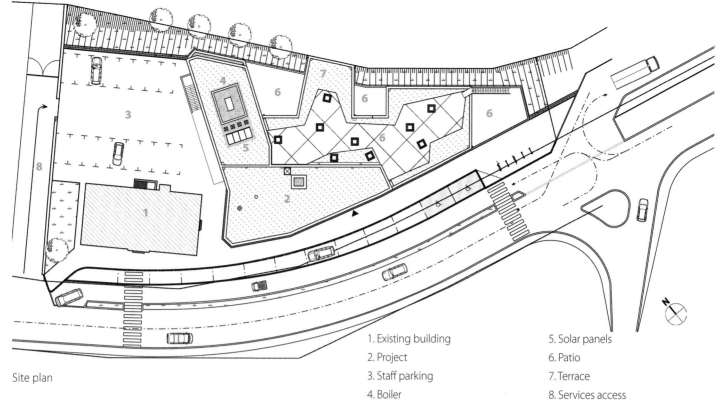

Site plan

1. Existing building
2. Project
3. Staff parking
4. Boiler

5. Solar panels
6. Patio
7. Terrace
8. Services access

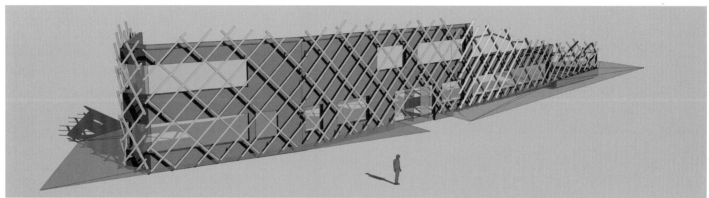

GROUND FLOOR PLAN

1. Entrance	5. Child washrooms	9. Office	13. Classroom	17. Classroom	21. Motor room
2. Lobby	6. Cleaning area	10. Dining room	14. Rest area	18. Storeroom	22. Art room
3. Management office	7. Garbage area	11. Laundry	15. Patio	19. Babies´ room	23. Water games
4. Staff washroom	8. Changing room	12. Washroom	16. Toy storeroom	20. Bottle room	24. Kitchen

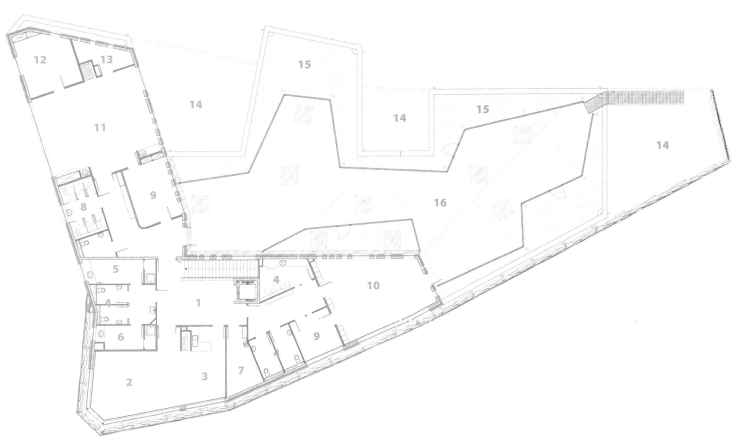

FIRST FLOOR

1. Hall	5. Women´s changeroom	9. Office	13. Storeroom
2. Meeting room	6. Men´s changeroom	10. Multiuse room	14. Lower deck
3. Staff rest area	7. Cleaning area	11. Activities	15. Green roof
4. Washrooms	8. Children´s washrooms	12. Rest area	16. Patio

SECTION

1. M. dressing room
2. Shower
3. Kitchen

4. Cleaning area
5. Lobby
6. Arts center

7. Motor room
8. Washrooms
9. Multipurpose room

10. Terrace

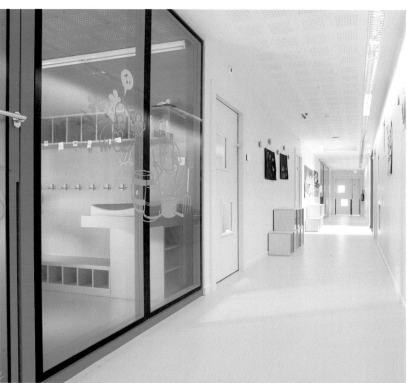

On the inside, studs and suspended acoustic ceilings are all in plasterboard, and the floor heating system is covered with a rubber floor.

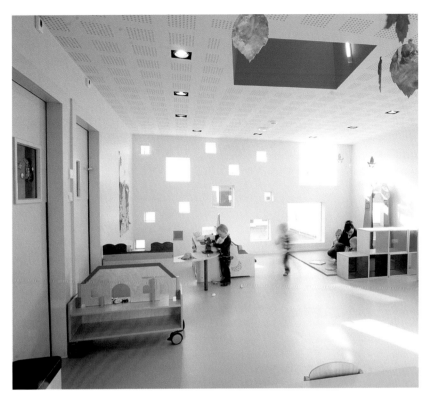

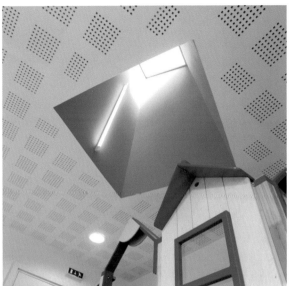

g.o.y.a. (group of young architects)

Freispiel

Guntramsdorf, Austria

Photographs: Kurt Hörbst

Freispiel kindergarten is located in a beautiful setting, nestled in a grove of chestnut trees. Its rustic design celebrates a sense of open space and connection with its environment.

To meet the various needs of the children the building is organized as a series of structures, each connected visually with the trees. Classrooms are arranged around a hallway which, like the activity area, branches out from the foyer. Clad in larch wood, and with floor to ceiling windows affording panoramic views of the surroundings, the foyer was designed as a multi-purpose area that provides additional space to enable different kinds of activities to take place simultaneously in the various sections of the building. The wall it shares with the gymnasium is flexible and can be folded back to create a larger, open events room when needed.

The interior of the building is also clad in larch wood to harmonize with the environment. Load bearing walls of spruce cross-laminated timber are faced with triple-layered spruce panels finished with a bright white varnish.Each classroom has a large panoramic window set at child's-eye level with ample lower sills that double as benches. In contrast to the airy classrooms, the gallery offers a more intimate experience; light floods in from a skylight through which the tops of trees can be glimpsed.

The upright trunks of the old trees around the kindergarten suggest strength and perseverance, and these characteristics are expressed in the language of the building with its preponderance of wood. Footbridges and terraces link the classrooms, imparting a sense of well-being.Three themed play areas – Balance and Equilibrium, Calm and Nature, and Sand and Water – are distributed around the garden of the property.

Conceived as a low-energy building, the school is heated in winter and cooled in summer by a ground water heat pump feeding under floor piping. CO_2 concentration controlled ventilation ensures optimum air quality.

Architecture:
g.o.y.a. (group of young architects)
Project leader:
Paul JE Preiss
General planner:
ARGE KS + g.o.y.a.
Site area:
3,600 sqm (39,200 sqft)
Project area:
730 sqm (7,900 sqft)

Designed as a multi-purpose area, the foyer provides additional space to enable different kinds of activities to take place simultaneously in the various sections of the building, but the wall it shares with the gymnasium is flexible and can be folded back to create a larger, open events room.

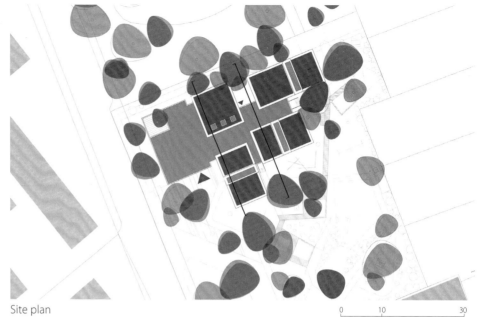

Site plan

0   10   30

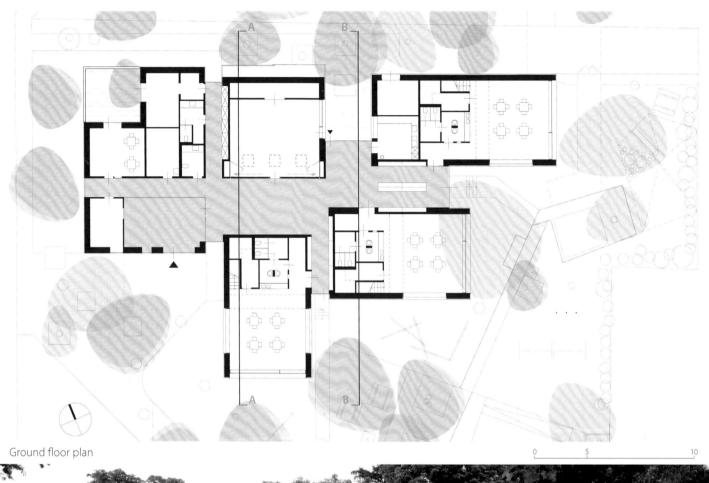

Ground floor plan

0   5   10

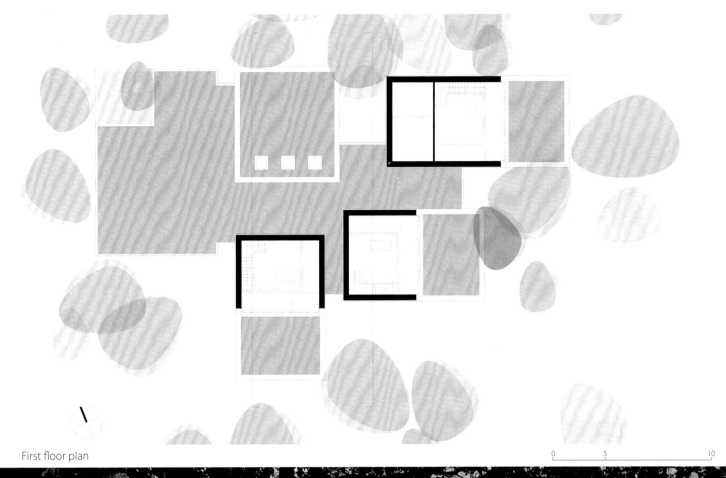

First floor plan

0   5   10

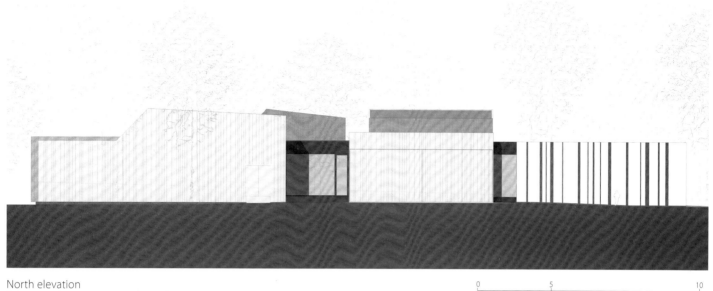

North elevation

0 5 10

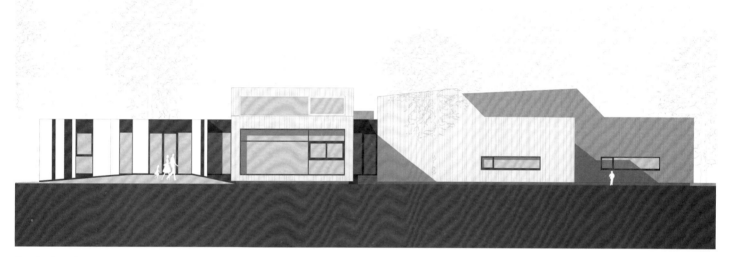

South elevation

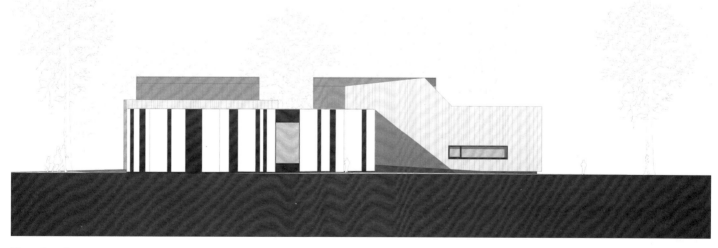

West elevation

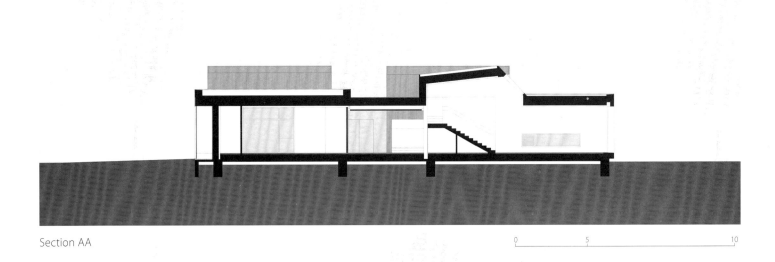

Section AA

0   5   10

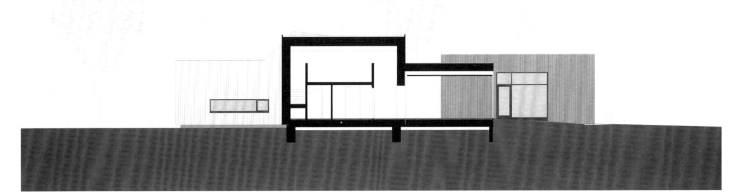

Section BB

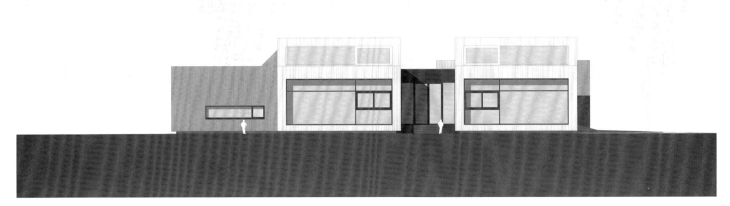

East elevation

The interior of the building is clad in larch wood to harmonize with the environment. Load bearing walls of spruce cross-laminated timber are faced with triple-layered spruce panels finished with a bright white varnish.

The upright trunks of the old trees around the kindergarten suggest strength and perseverance, and these characteristics are expressed in the language of the building with its preponderance of wood.

Paredes Pedrosa arquitectos

Universidad Popular Infantil. UPI Gandía

Gandía, Spain

Photographs: Roland Halbe, Luis Asín

The Childrens' University in Gandía (UPI) is an experimental initiative proposed by the Municipality of Gandía. The UPI is not a conventional kindergarten, but a group of specialized classrooms and workshops located in a natural setting where children can develop their creativity and have fun beyond a school context. The proposed volume does not alter the Ausías March Park's layout. Indeed, it respects the position of six existing white mulberry trees, arranging the classrooms around them and shaping a central courtyard. This courtyard is the core of the Childrens' University, linking open spaces, covered areas and indoor rooms. Towards the exterior, the building exhibits a sober and continuous façade, serving as a sort of palisade, that avoids building up fences. White colored ceramic tiles build up both façades and roof.

There is continuity in the material that builds up the whole exterior of the building. From the outside, the building seems to be a light, white ceramic fence where the shade of the nearby trees is reflected. Vernacular architecture in this Mediterranean area uses ceramic that does not need any maintenance and adapts naturally to its mild climate. In summer it reflects the strong local light and protects inside from high temperatures.

Ceramics are designed as three-dimensional pieces with a can-shaped mold that resembles a continuous bamboo fence. The pieces are double faced and the flat side is used for the roof. In the patio, the façades are built with wooden carpentries painted white, so there is a transparency between the interior and exterior and all mulberry trees can be seen from the classrooms. Indoors, linoleum floors and cork ceilings help absorb sound and are combined with the concrete structure walls.

The building's very concept contributes to sustainability. Due to a tight budget, the building was designed to accommodate sustainable practices in the architecture itself. The interior is shaded from the intense summer sun by the mulberry trees that attenuate solar irradiation and cast scattered shadows to the interior of classrooms. This also reduces the need of artificial lights to the essentials. In winter, meanwhile, the mulberry trees lose their leaves allowing sunlight to freely enter the classrooms. When spring arrives the trees are transformed and provide natural shade.

Architecture:
Paredes Pedrosa arquitectos
(Ángela García de Paredes, Ignacio Pedrosa)
Collaborators:
Álvaro Oliver, Álvaro Rábano,
Lucía Guadalajara, Ángel Camacho,
Laura Pacheco
Project Management:
Antonio García Blay
Structure:
Alfonso G. Gaite. GOGAITE, S.L.
Installations:
JG Ingenieros
Ceramics:
Ceràmica Cumella
Client:
Ayuntamiento de Gandía
Built area:
1,100sqm (12,000 sqft)

Site plan

1. Ducal Palace of the Borgias
2. Jesuit College
3. Convent of Santa Clara
4. San Marcos Hospital
5. Gandia City Hall
6. Collegiate Church of Santa María
7. Church of the Blessed
8. Serpis River
9. River lookout

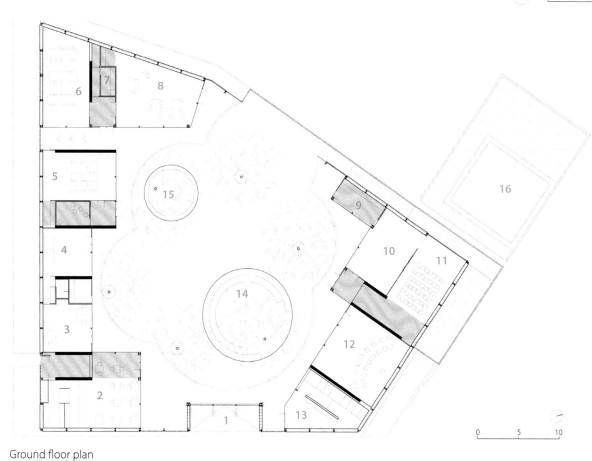

Ground floor plan

1. Entrance
2. Cafeteria
3. Office
4. Baby room
5. Reading room
6. Computer room
7. Photography
8. Painting and drawing
9. Dressing room
10. Dancing
11. Theatre
12. Music room
13. Rest room
14. Open air theatre
15. Sand pit
16. Swimming basin

Site plan: before

1. 6 existing mulberry trees
2. Upi school
3. Swimming pool in former park basin

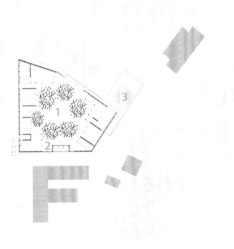

Site plan: after

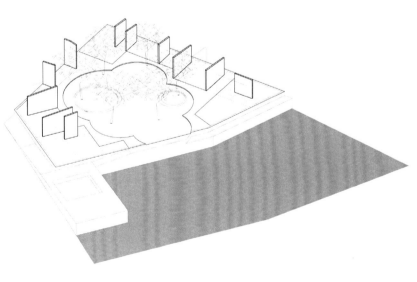

Axonometric view

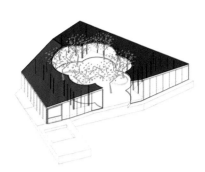

Natural lighting
Interior glass façade in patio provides maximum natural light. 6 existing mulberry trees carpet the ground with leaves in the winter.

Shading protected glass façade
Cantilevered eaves. The mulberry trees provide shade in summer.

Water balance within Ausías March Parc, patio with unsealed tamped soil. Evaporation and direct rainwater release.

Climatic control, patio with unsealed tamped soil. Evaporation and cross-ventilation.

Irradiation control: ventilated ceramic tiles on the façade and white ceramic tiles on the roof provide sun protection.

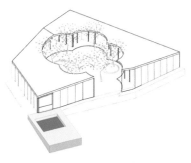

Existing water basin adapted into a children´s pool.∫

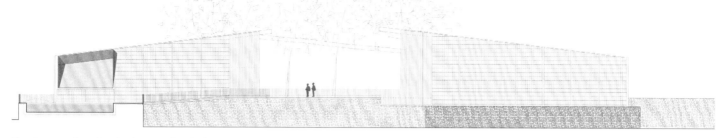

North-west elevation, lookout to Serpis river

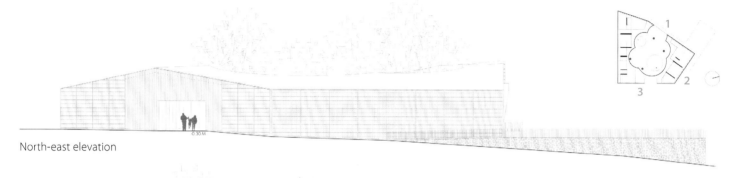

North-east elevation

±0.00

East elevation, main entrance

1. North-west elevation
2. North-east elevation
3. East elevation

The UPI is not a conventional kindergarten, but a group of specialized classrooms and workshops located in a natural setting where children can develop their creativity and have fun beyond a school context.

Section 3: computer room, painting, dancing and theatre

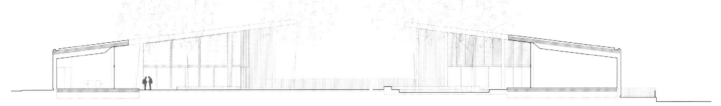

Section 2: office and classrooms

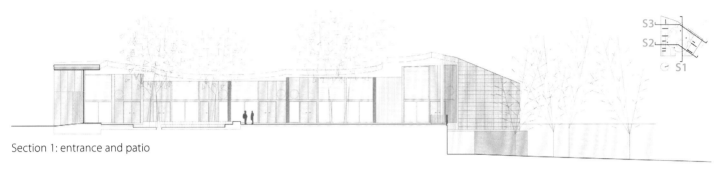

Section 1: entrance and patio

The building is designed to respect and incorporate the presence of six white mulberry trees in the park, which are integrated aesthetically with the children's university and also provide shade in the summer.

209

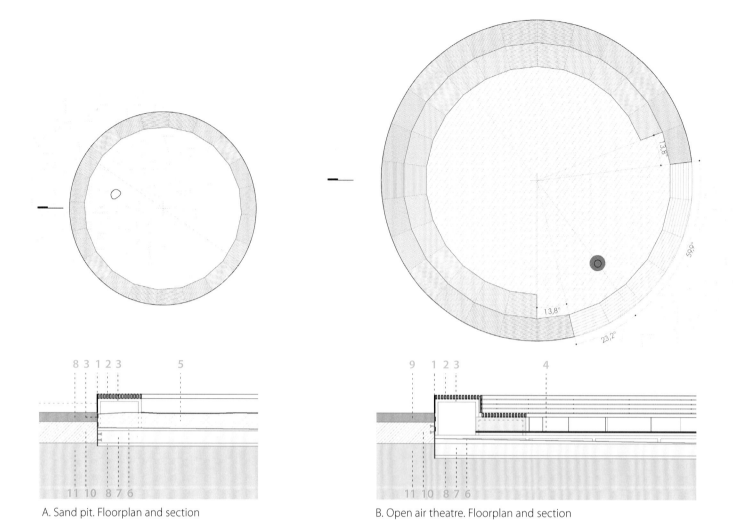

A. Sand pit. Floorplan and section

B. Open air theatre. Floorplan and section

1. Earth retention perimetral cylinder 10mm curved steel plate

2. Decking fronts and seats 7x2, 5 cm, variable length section pieces

3. Structure of 50x50x3 hollow steel bracket for wood paneling and welded to perimetral steel cylinder, acting as a buttress

4. Horizontal floor decking. Variable length sections with metal substructure

5. Sandbox

6. Light concrete for sloping

7. 20cm concrete slab

8. Blinding concrete, 5cm

9. Earthware pavement, 15cm

10. Compacted aggregates, 25cm

11. Exisiting land

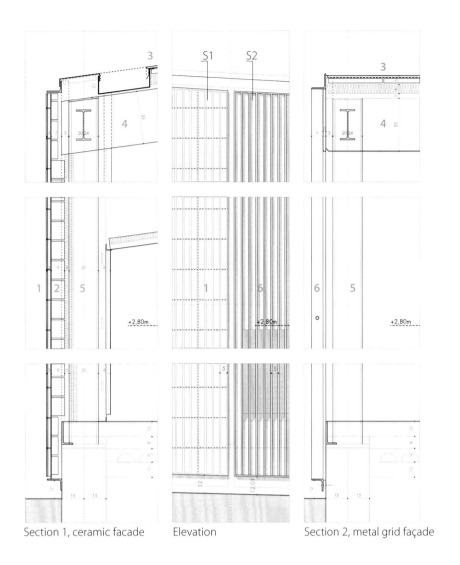

Section 1, ceramic facade   Elevation   Section 2, metal grid façade

1. Ventilated white ceramic tile

2. Brick base

3. White ceramic tile as roof cladding

4. Concrete structure roof slab

5. Metal structure

6. Metal grid

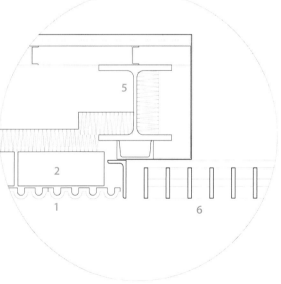

Horizontal section

Tham & Videgård Arkitekter

Tellus Nursery School

Telefonplan, Stockholm, Sweden

Photographs: Åke E:son Lindman, Lindman Photography

This nursery school mediates between different contexts and scales, located as it is on the border between a former industrial development and a small forest where new housing is being developed. The first space greeting parents and children when they arrive is a semi-enclosed courtyard at the entrace, whose organic layout encourages movement, leading into the rest of the building, where space becomes continuous and creates both exterior and itnerior rooms of challenging shapes. Windows are freely placed at different heights to allow for light and for the views to be adapted to both an adult's and a child's point of view. This reinforces the relationship between the interior and the exterior playgrounds and the wooded hill beyond.

Together with the client and the pedagogical inspiration taken from the Reggio Emilia school, a new way to organize the interior was developed. The result is a rather unorthodox plan, where instead of a complete 'flat' for each group of children, there will be a large common interior plaza where the six groups can interact around different activities, play opportunities and learning projects. This main space is complemented with separate atelier spaces for water projects and art, as well as some small, secluded group rooms for rest and quiet activities.

The façade panel, made of 50x50mm sawn wood, filters direct sunlight into the nursery school and create hidden windows that underscores the curved interior and exterior spaces. The building complies with the highest standards for environmentally friendly and long term sound construction.

Architecture:
Tham & Videgård Arkitekter
Chief architects:
Bolle Tham and Martin Videgård
Project architect:
Eric Engström
Collaborators:
Mårten Nettelbladt, Johan Björkholm,
Karolina Nyström, Marcus Andrén,
Julia Schönbrunn, Andreas Helgesson
Client:
Vasakronan AB
User:
City council of Hägersten-Liljeholmen
Total built area:
1,200 sqm (13,000 sqft)
Site area:
1,700 sqm (18,300 sqft)

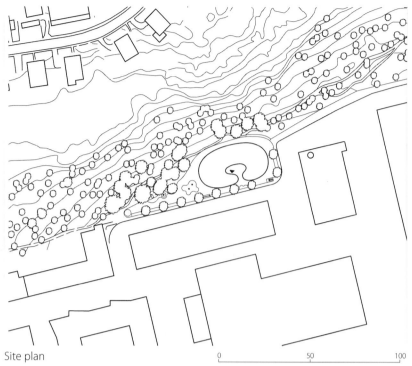

Site plan

0   50   100

Windows are freely placed at different heights to allow for light and for the views to be adapted to both an adult's and a child's point of view. This reinforces the relationship between the interior and the exterior playgrounds and the wooded hill beyond.

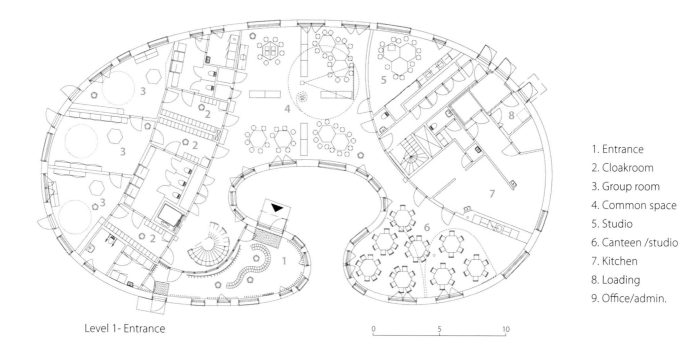

Level 1- Entrance

1. Entrance
2. Cloakroom
3. Group room
4. Common space
5. Studio
6. Canteen /studio
7. Kitchen
8. Loading
9. Office/admin.

0   5   10

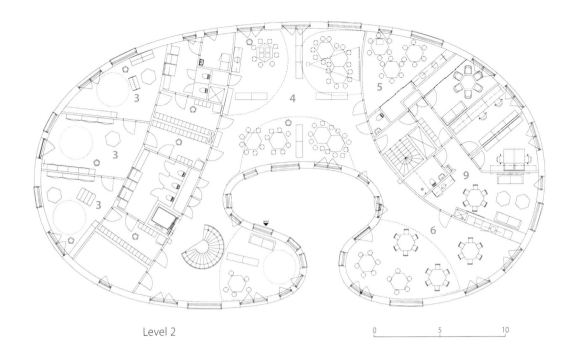

Level 2

0   5   10

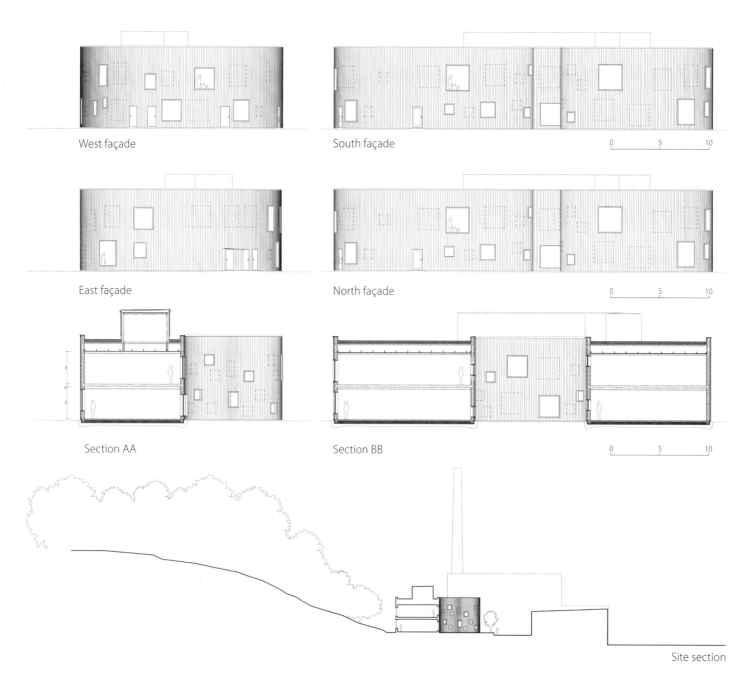

West façade

South façade

0 5 10

East façade

North façade

0 5 10

Section AA

Section BB

0 5 10

Site section

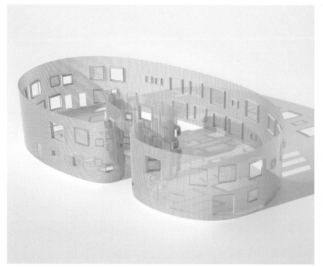

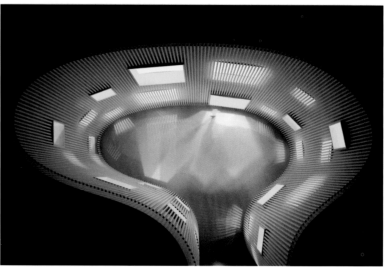

Horizontal section through façade

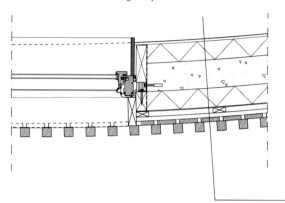

50x50 vertical sawn wood panel
22x100 wooden boards
22x100 k-plywood
28x70 battens
4 fibre cementboard
100 insulation
150 concrete
100 insulation

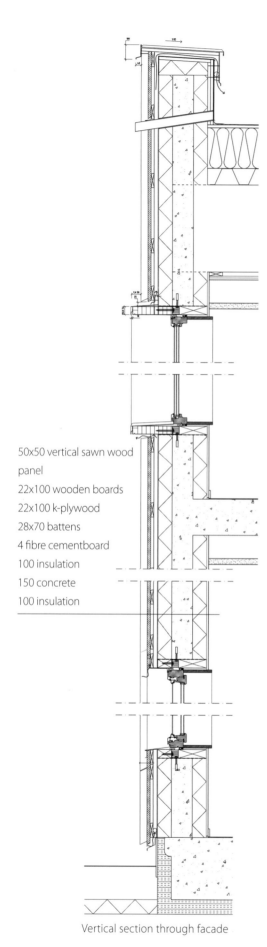

50x50 vertical sawn wood
panel
22x100 wooden boards
22x100 k-plywood
28x70 battens
4 fibre cementboard
100 insulation
150 concrete
100 insulation

Vertical section through facade

Van Rooijen Nourbakhsh Architecten

Playground Building

Utrecht, the Netherlands

Photographs: Cornbread Works

This playground building was designed and built by Dutch architecture studio Van Rooijen Nourbakhsh, an office that combines a practical approach with a preference for conceptual designs, craftsmanship and aesthetics

The site is located in an inner courtyard in the district of Oudwijk, right in the heart of the city of Utrecht. The building that originally stood in this place had become worn and tatty and so in order to rejuvenate the area's inner-city landscape, the town council decided to commission the architects to design a playground for the children of the neighborhood.

The brief called for a modest, durable and safe building that would upgrade the original playground and appeal to children. The building has separate spaces for a kindergarten, a playroom, an office and storage.

The creative solution that was applied to the project consists of a series of movable partitions that enable the different spaces to be interlinked and thus provide space for a range of different activities and multiple uses. In this way the play space can also be made suitable for different age groups.

The building's simple, rectangular structure has been clad in wood and given a playful sculptural finish by way of irregular, glazed openings and bright and cheerful colors. The windows combine with outdoor canopies to blur the boundaries between the interior and exterior play area, strengthening the relationship between the two spaces.

The building has many small features which are connected with the perception of children: a glass corner that gives children the sensation they are playing outside; a roof window, which is exciting to sit beneath when it rains; and an edge of soil around the perimeter of the building, which serves to protect the structure, but also for the children to grow plants in.

Architecture:
Van Rooijen Nourbakhsh Architecten
Client:
Municipality of Utrecht

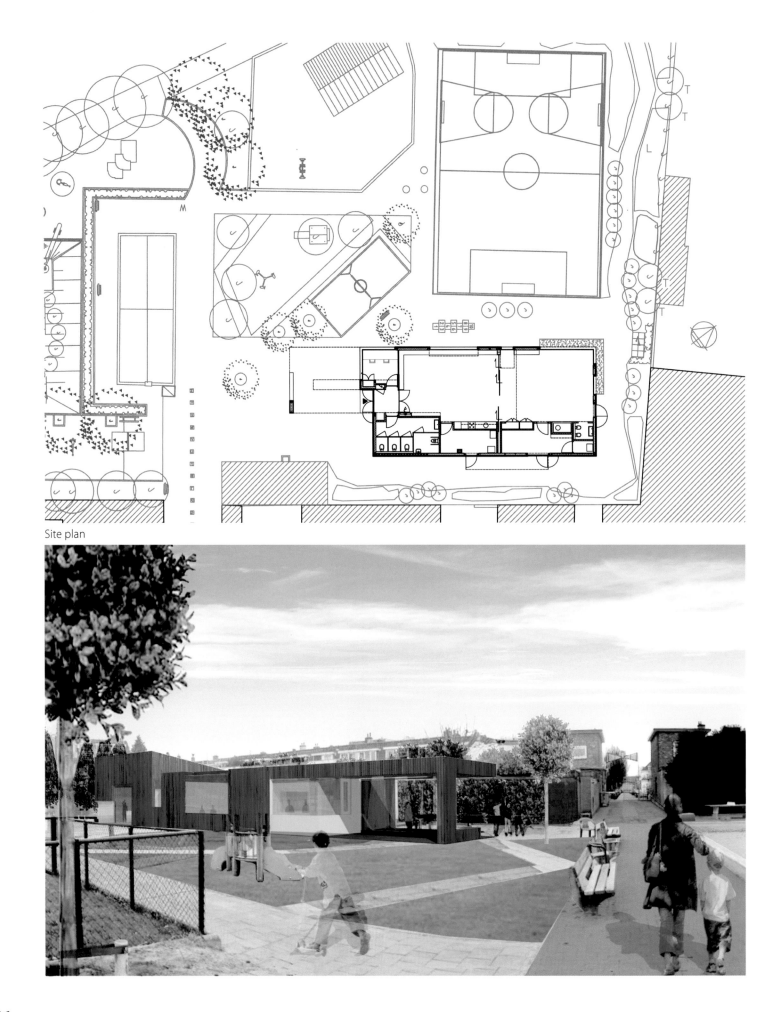

Site plan

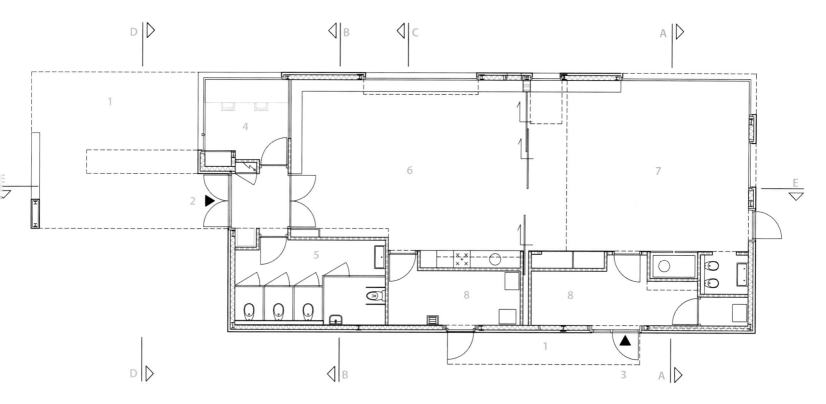

FLOOR PLAN

1. Canopy	3. Entrance daycare	5. Washrooms	7. Daycare
2. Entrance	4. Office	6. Playroom	8. Storage

The building's simple, rectangular structure has been clad in wood and given a playful sculptural finish by way of irregular, glazed openings and bright and cheerful colors.

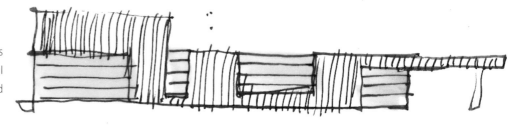

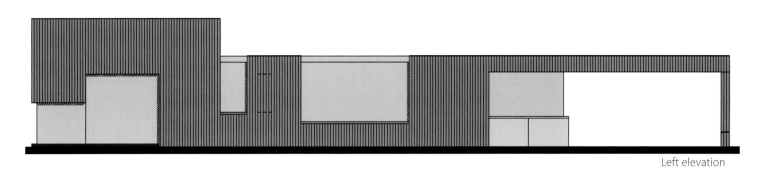

Left elevation

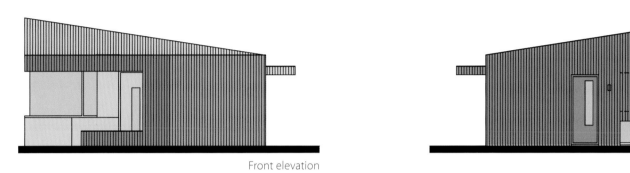

Front elevation

Rear elevation

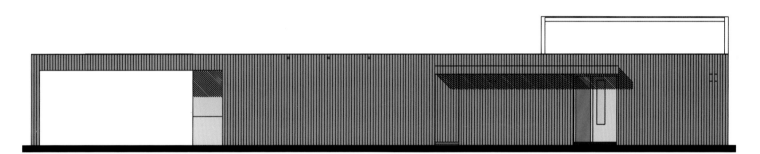

Right elevation

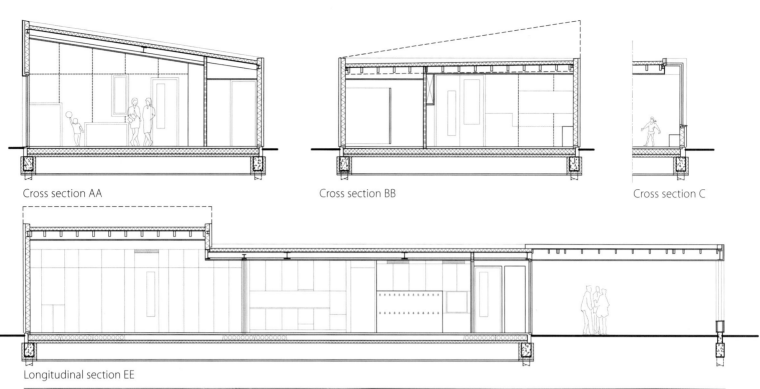

Cross section AA   Cross section BB   Cross section C

Longitudinal section EE

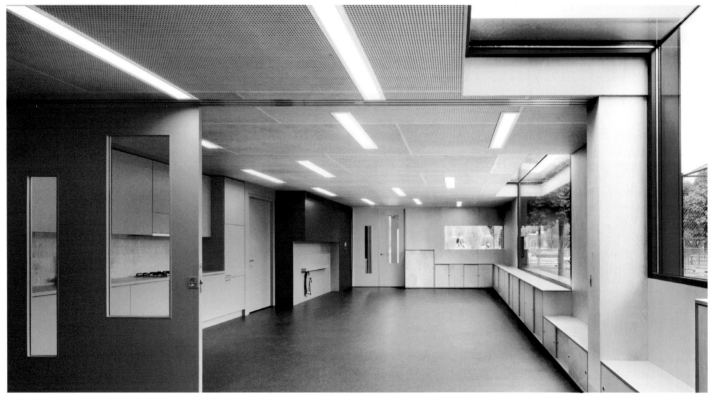

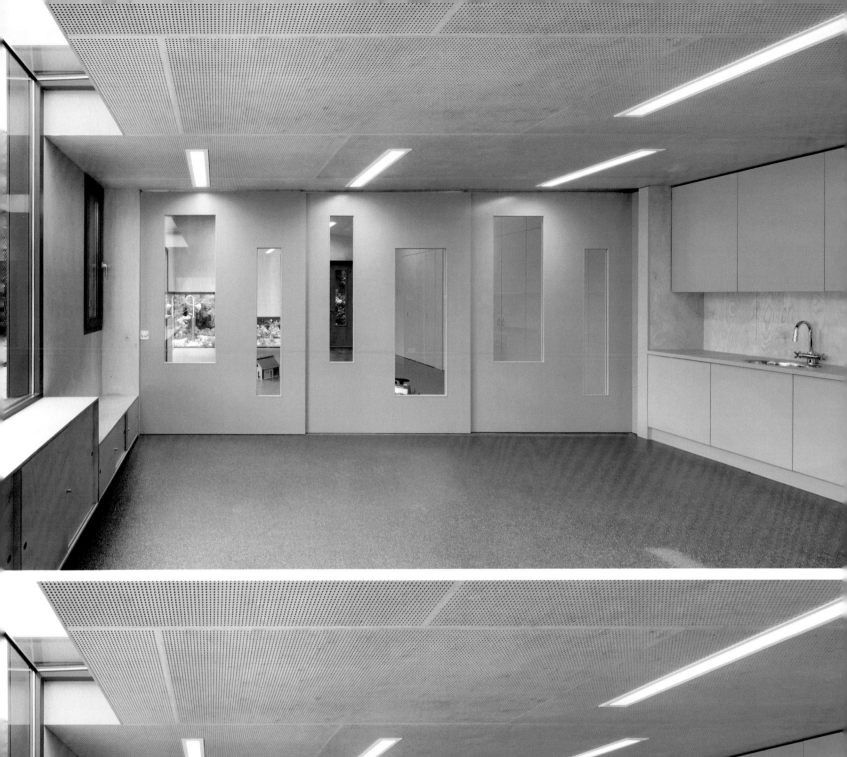

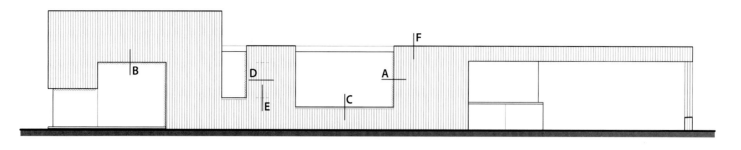

KEY

1. Multiplex
2. Aluminium profile
3. Wooden window frame
4. Mounted enameled colored aluminum
5. Ventilation openings in wooden lattice
6. Wooden lath
7. Steel beam

B

C

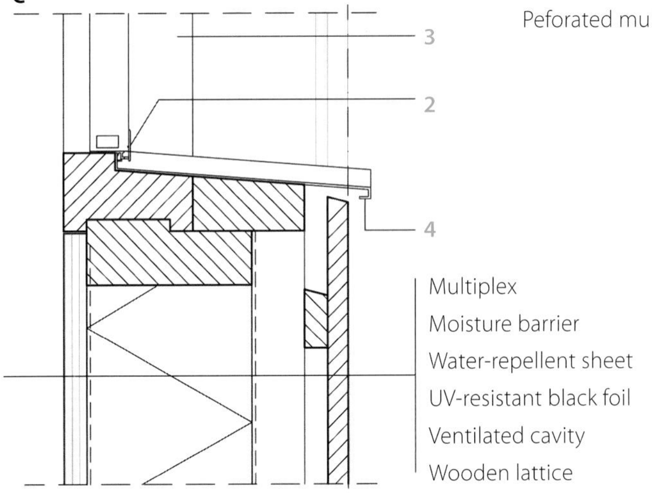

3

2

4

Multiplex
Moisture barrier
Water-repellent sheet
UV-resistant black foil
Ventilated cavity
Wooden lattice

D

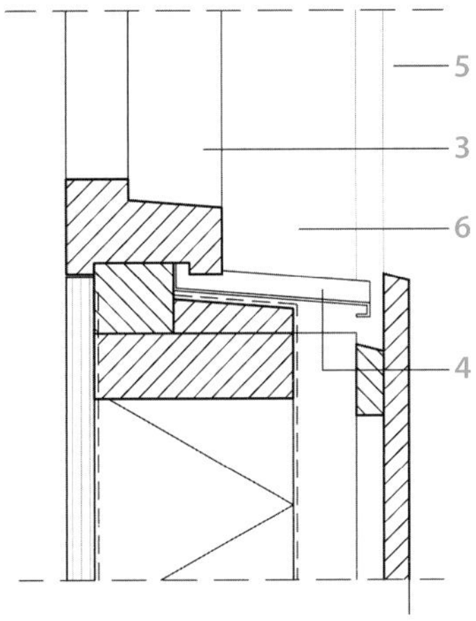

5

3

6

4

F

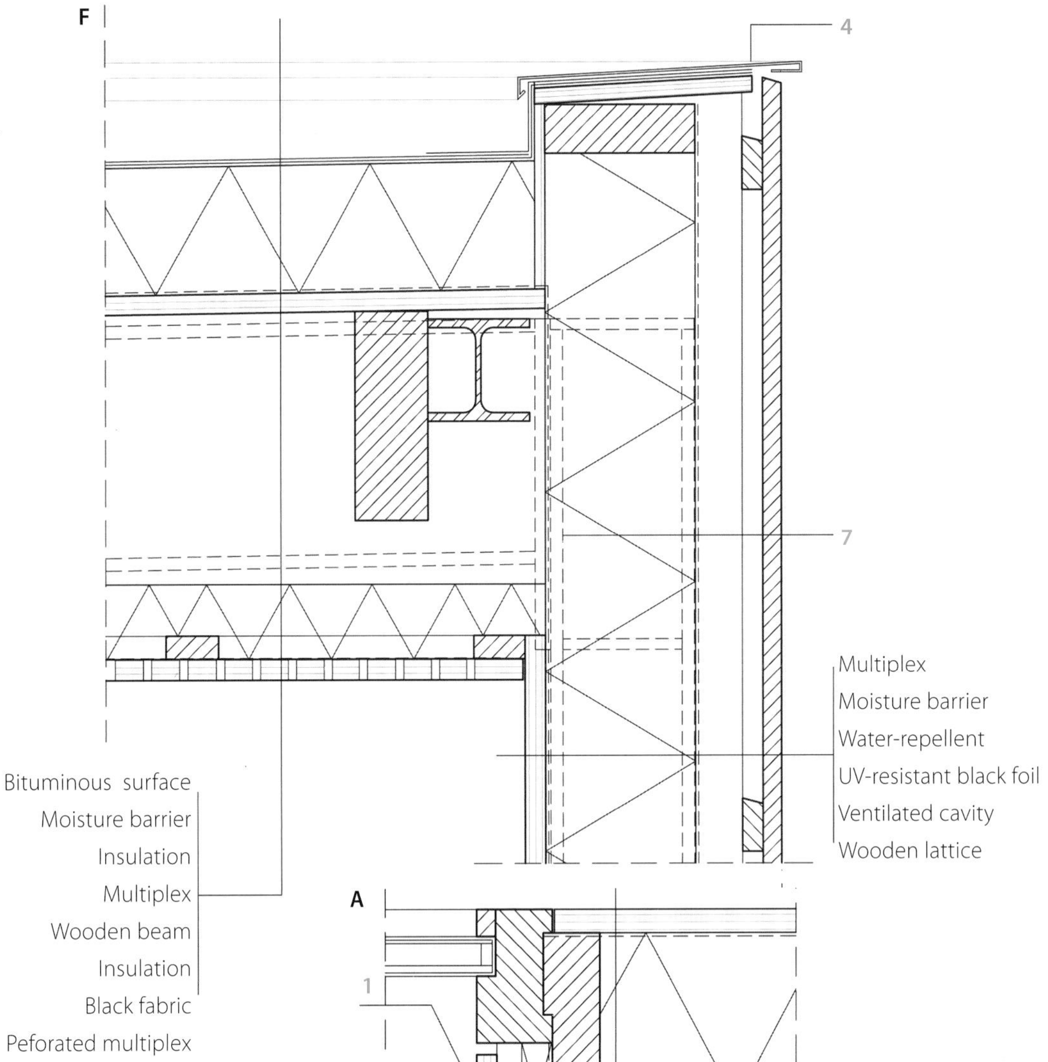

4

7

Multiplex
Moisture barrier
Water-repellent
UV-resistant black foil
Ventilated cavity
Wooden lattice

Bituminous surface
Moisture barrier
Insulation
Multiplex
Wooden beam
Insulation
Black fabric
Peforated multiplex

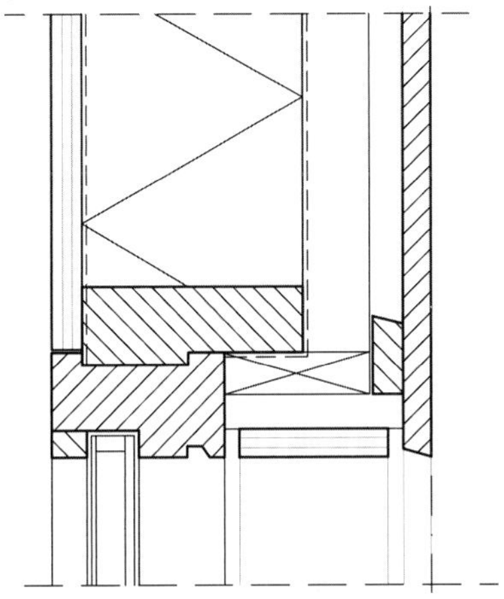

A

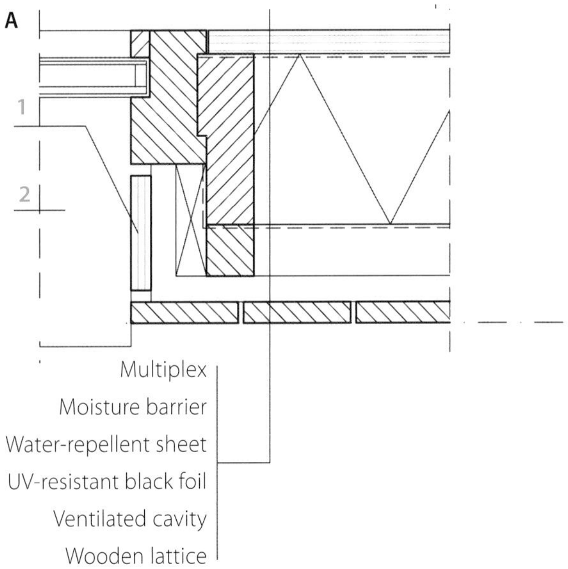

1

2

Multiplex
Moisture barrier
Water-repellent sheet
UV-resistant black foil
Ventilated cavity
Wooden lattice

E

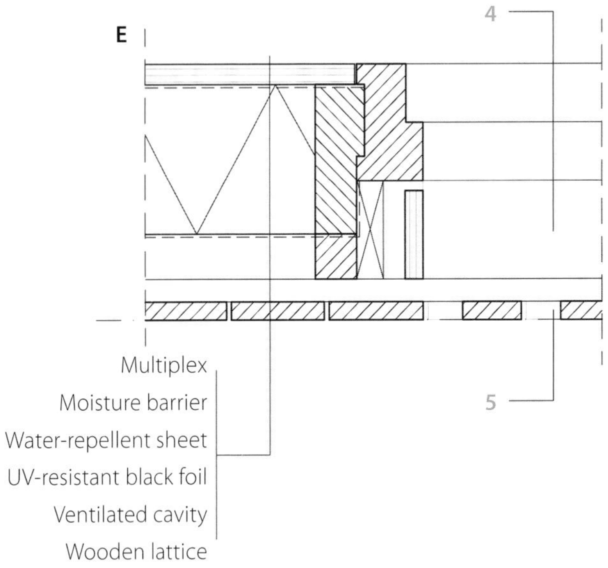

4

5

Multiplex
Moisture barrier
Water-repellent sheet
UV-resistant black foil
Ventilated cavity
Wooden lattice

233

Giancarlo Mazzanti

Timayui Kindergarten

Timayui, Santa Marta, Colombia

Photographs: contributed by Giancarlo Mazzanti

This project, backed by the municipality of Santa Marta and the Carulla Foundation, aimed to develop an installation to help vulnerable children in a low-income neighborhood on the outskirts of the city, an area characterized by violence and lack of public infrastructure. The enterprise encourages children, assists in their development and provides them with a balanced diet.

The challenge for the architects was to design a project that generated social inclusion, could be used in multiple ways, and would become an element of pride and transformation in the community. The building is conceived as a visible structure representing a symbol of the neighborhood, designed to relate to the geography of the region and the topography of the site.

The architects created an open, adaptable system comprised of modules which were arranged to look like a chain of flowers, each with a trio of petals, and were distributed to make maximum use of the lot. The three-armed structures all have a large, open courtyard at the center which creates a smooth connection between the interior and exterior. Each module contains bathrooms, two preschool classrooms and an open sensory room connected to the yard in order to develop an educational continent identifiable by the children. The modules can be adapted to other uses such as a dining room and a kitchen. There are also indoor play areas, covered outdoor zones and various playgrounds. Garden spaces have been created to promote native ecosystem education through the planting and care of indigenous plants.

The buildings have a concrete bearing wall system for easy implementation and rapid construction. These walls act as support membranes, replacing the columns and beams of a traditional supporting system, and create 4 m (13 ft) overhangs at the end of the classrooms. The walls are covered with ceramic elementsto make maintenance and cleaning of the building easier.

Sustainable features of the project include a heat-regulating system – the thermally efficientfaçade with natural ventilation – which avoids the need for air conditioning and reduces energy consumption, the materials used minimized the amount of waste, so lowering environmental impact, and the north-south orientation of the buildings allows for natural ventilation and natural lighting. There are gardens for urban agriculture, recycled rain and waste water are used for the bathrooms and for irrigation, and kitchen waste is composted. Waste recycling is done on site and delivered to the collection system, lowering the cost of this service and at the same time generating income through the sale of recyclable materials.

The project is socially committed, implementing agriculture and productivity as a thematic complement to the development of educational activities, and giving the community and the individuals the opportunity to be productive for their own benefit.The architects created the installation with a view to the future and the integration of more children, and the modular design allows for more units to be added. The system is characterized by flexible, neutral spaces which allow for a wide variety of activities, and the close relation between the interior and exterior spaces promotes the development of good relationships between all the children and their teachers.

Architecture:
Giancarlo Mazzanti
Design team:
Susana Somoza,
Andrés Sarmiento,
Néstor Gualteros, Oscar Cano,
Lucia Largo
Area:
1,450 sqm (15,608 sqft)

1. Access
2. Administration
3. Kitchen
4. Refectory
5. Material
6. Silent sensory space
7. First steps
8. Creative movement sensory space
9. Light & shadow sensory space
10. Toddles
11. Pre-kindergarten
12. Sound sensory space
13. Kindergarten 1
14. Art studio
15. Kindergarten 2
16. Expansion area
17. Administration 2nd floor
18. Farm yard
19. Sand yard
20. Orchard yard
21. Yard
22. Flowers yard
23. Leaves yard

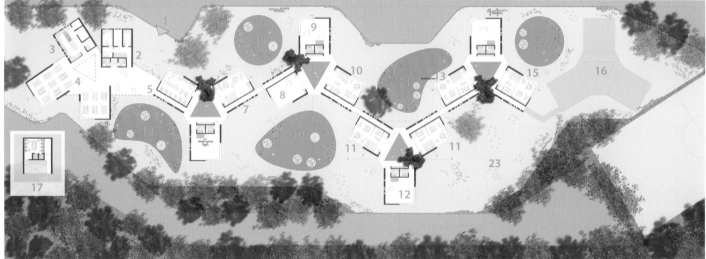

General plan

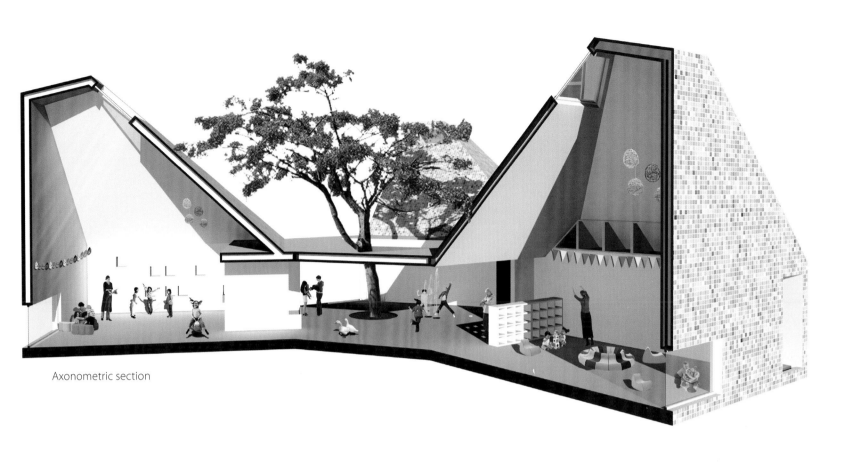

Axonometric section

In addition to the classrooms there are also indoor play areas, covered outdoor zones and various playgrounds. Garden spaces have been created to promote native ecosystem education through the planting and care of indigenous plants.

CLASSROOM

1. Assembly
2. Water and sand
3. Art
4. Light & shadow
5. Writing & reading
6. Construction

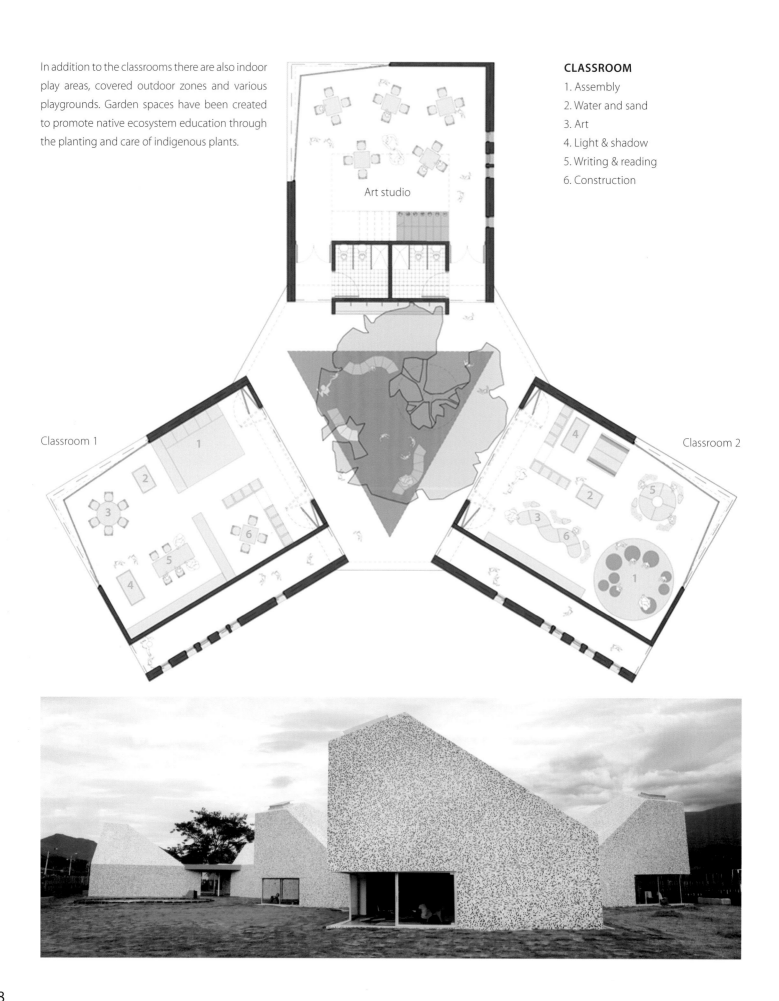

Art studio

Classroom 1

Classroom 2

The project is socially committed, implementing agriculture and productivity as a thematic complement to the development of educational activities, and giving the community and the individuals the opportunity to be productive for their own benefit.

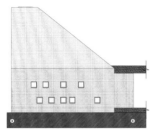

Elevation 1A

Elevation 2A

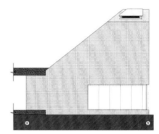

Elevation 3A

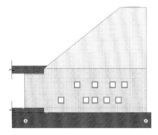

Elevation 1B

Elevation 2B

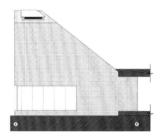

Elevation 3B

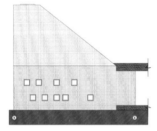

Elevation 1C

Elevation 2C

Elevation 2D

Section 1

Section 2

Section 3

Section 4

Section 5

Section 6

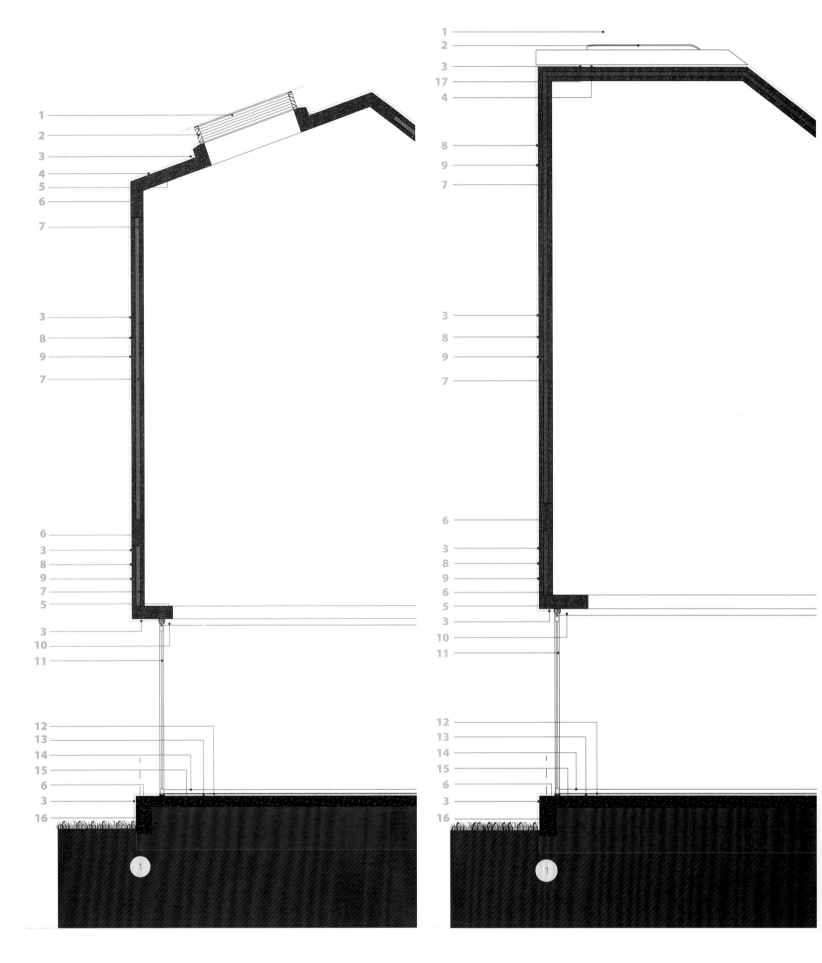

1

1

1. Laminated tempered glass and opalization for skylight
2. Aluminum skylight blind
3. Ground glass mosaic
4. Waterproofing
5. Metal plate with rust and synthetic enamlel finish
6. Gray concrete beam
7. Structural wall panels made of corrugated structural core of expanded polystyrene, galvanized steel wire mesh at each side of the core and two layers of mortar
8. Low absorption adhesive mortar for ceramic elements in gray or white
9. Nozzle for ground glass mosaic
10. Profile with hung top rail
11. Tempered glass
12. PVC slab
13. Leveling mortar
14. Lower profile on guide
15. Solid concrete slab
16. Gray concrete structural wall
17. Cover panels made of corrugated structural core of expanded polystyrene, galvanized steel wire mesh at each side of the core and two layers of mortar
18. Beam foundation or mooring
19. Sliding glass door
20. 5mm tempered glass
21. Clamping profiles for small glass windows in façade
22. Pisa glass anodized aluminum profiles

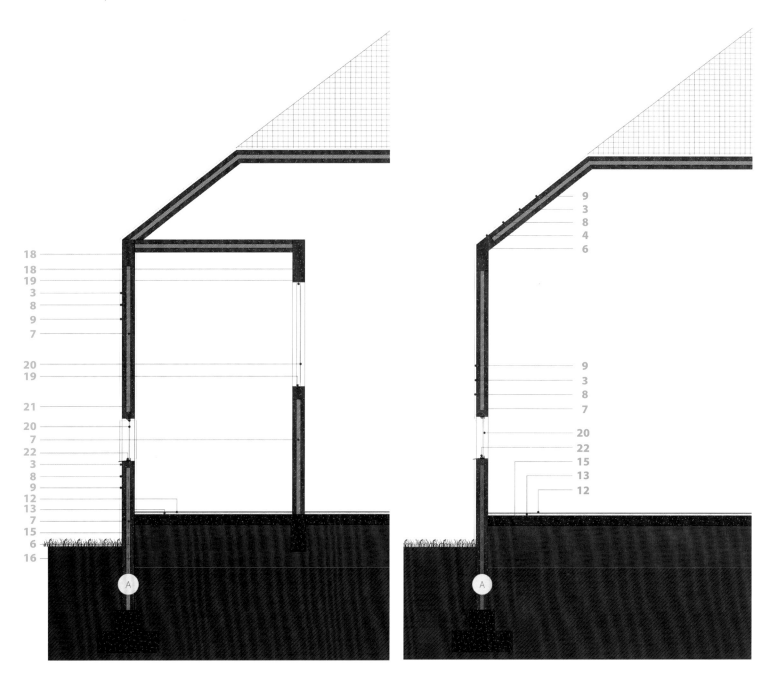

av62arquitectos slp

Kindergarden Turonet

Cerdanyola del Vallès, Spain

Photographs: Nico Baumgarten

This project grew from the committment to provide small children with a pleasant and stimulating space, spacially and sensually appropriate to the particular relationship that such young children have with their surroundings, which is much more based on touch and smell than upon visual characteristics.

The idea was to design spaces that would be discovered with the hands, with the body. Walls that could be touched and climbed in safety. Furniture that the children could move and alter and use in play. Places with their own little corners. Places that demanded to be explored and examined. A spatial distribution that allows the children to explore and create their own space. The children begin by making their classrooms their own, and then the patios.. and then they discover the children in the other classes, and finally the garden.

The garden is fundamental to the project. Different areas are identified and distinguished by different types of Mediterranean trees. There will be a corner for oranges, for olives, for carob, and for holm oak. In the steepest areas, not intended to be accessible to the children, a dense vegetation of fragrant Mediterranean bushes has been planted: lavender, thyme, rosemary, mastic, cistus, and broom. The aim is that the children, from an early age, should have direct contact with natural cycles.

The building is constructed so as to take advantage of the land and to adapt, with as little impact as possible, a rather large program onto only one floor. The pedestrian entrance is off of Pompeu Fabra street, and from Castillejos street there is a separate access ramp. The main façade is parallel to Lesseps street.

The steep slopes of the surrounding streets have made it necessary to put in retaining walls on the perimeter, which in the end contribute to the outward appearance of the building. Part of the building is constructed of walls built perpendicular to the longitudinal axis of the plot, which are covered with a flat roof with skylights. There are 7 classrooms in the space created by parallel walls, equipped with the necessary services for each age bracket. The other spaces of the program are located under the unifying flat roof, which extends to the limits of the plot of land.

Inside, the building is bright and lit in an indirect and controlled manner by the skylights.

Architecture:
av62arquitectos slp
Collaborating Architect:
Blanca Pujals, Architect
Client:
Cerdanyola del Vallès Local Council
Area:
Total: 967 sqm (10,400 sqft)
Built:
685 sqm (7,400 sqft)

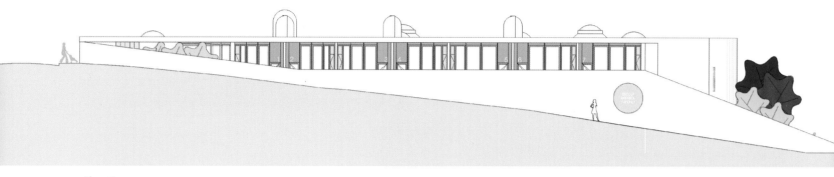

Elevation

This project grew from the commitment to provide small children with a pleasant and stimulating space, specially and sensually appropriate to the particular relationship that such young children have with their surroundings, which is much more based on touch and smell than upon visual characteristics. The building is constructed so as to take advantage of the land and to adapt, with as little impact as possible, a rather large program onto only one floor. The garden is fundamental to the project. Different areas are identified and distinguished by different types of Mediterranean trees.

Part of the building is constructed of walls built perpendicular to the longitudinal axis of the plot, which are covered with a flat roof with skylights. There are 7 classrooms in the space created by parallel walls, equipped with the necessary services for each age bracket.

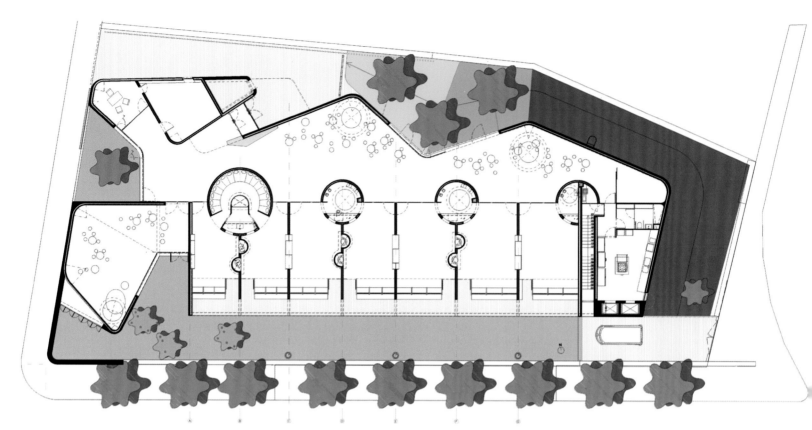

Ground floor plan

1. Polyurethane water-proofing system

2. Sloped mortar layer

3. Extruded polystyrene

4. Vapor barrier

5. Reinforced concrete slab, 25 cm

6. Edge

7. Continuous rubber pavement

8. Glacomini underfloor heating

9. Insulating suspended floor plate

10. Air chamber

11. Geotextile

12. High density drainage sheet

13. 4 mm EPDH sheet, attached to exterior face of wall

14. Reinforced concrete wall, 25cm thick

15. Thermal insulation

16. Thermal clay

17. Concrete foundation

18. Blinding concrete

19. Gravel

20. 40cm diam. drainage tube

21. Sheet to cover galvanized steel roof, painted white

22. Glavanized steel anchoring piece

23. Drywall false ceiling

24. Brick walls

25. Mortar

26. Polyurethane mesh

27. Thermal insulation

28. DM registrable skylight cover

29. Natural finish woodword in Finnish pine

30. Interior panel in natural Finnish pine

31. Exterior panel in natural Finnish pine

32. DM blank side

33. Cement

34. Sloped mortar layer

35. Natural finish wooden struts, made of Finnish pine

36. Circular skylight, 200 cm diameter, polyester resin reinforced with fiberglass, with "sandwich" thermal insulation

37. Brick wall,10cm thick

38. Painted plaster

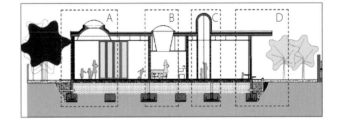

Detail A

Detail B

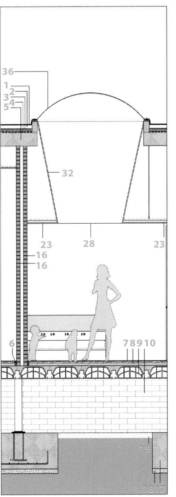

Detail C

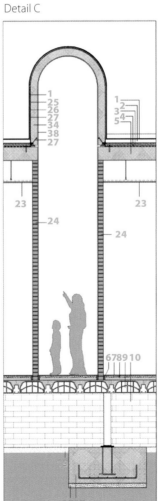

Detail D

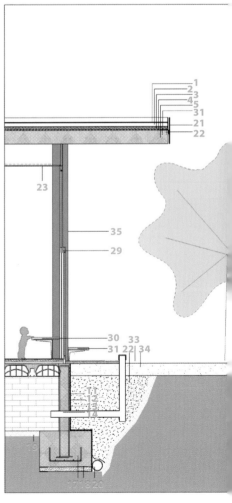

Paul Le Quernec

Childcare Facilities, Boulay and Piblange

Boulay and Piblange, France

Photographs: Paul Le Quernec

This project, lauched by "La communauté de communes du Pays Boulageois" in 2010, was to simultaneously build two childcare centers, a childcare facility in Boulay and a micro-nursery in nearby Piblange of 900 sqm (9,700 sqft) and 300 sqm (3,600 sqft) respectively.

Despite the size difference between the two buildings, they both benefit from an open parcel of land and an urban context that imposes very few planning restrictions. The architects were thus able to explore a great contextual freedom and have been able to design these buildings by focusing on optimal functionality, safety and comfort, regardless of their size.

The concept arose from the idea that childcare facilities and nurseries are not intended for children but babies, which conditions the behavior and the sensitivity of the parents and the staff. The infants' fragility and need of protection were integrated into the architecture, which was developed as a uterine concept. This was only possible thanks to the unrestricted urban setting.

The entrance is set back from the street, away from traffic. In order to strengthen the visitors´ perception of feeling safe, it "submerges" into the building.

The interior of the building is organized around a highly protected circular central space. Children´s spaces gravitate and converge around this center. Views between each part of the building are centrifugal and centripedal. At the very center of the building, the circus tent-like wooden structure ends with a 3m (10ft) wide vaulted ceiling made of polycarbonate, which allows daylight in throughout the day.

Interior fittings are designed without right angles to produce smoothly curved walls, so as to make the space safer for its small occupants.

All exterior spaces are south-facing, to provide children with a playground protected from sun or rain. The roof of the building extends to cover these spaces, which can be used year round.

An added benefit of the centripetal organization is that it removes the requirement for extra hallways in the two buildings. Each childcare space is directly linked to the central area. This system saved the project about 100sqm (1,100 sqft), or a hallways raitio of about 11%. This allowed the two buildings to be designed to respect BBC (Low Energy-Use Building) regulations without going over-budget.

Architecture:
Paul Le Quernec

Structural Consultant:
HN ingénierie

Fluid Consultant:
Solares Bauen

Environmental consultant:
Solares Bauen

Construction economist:
E3 Economie

Client:
Communauté de Communes du Pays Boulageois

Floor area:
900 sqm (9,700 sqft) in Boulay
330 sqm (3,600 sqft) in Piblange

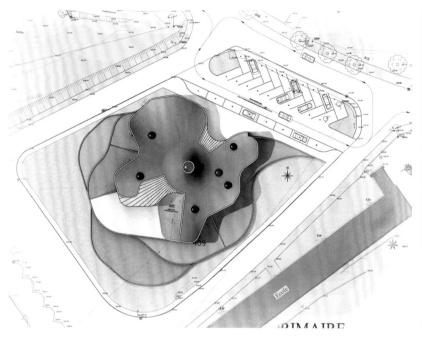

The architects were thus able to explore a great contextual freedom and have been able to design these buildings by focusing on optimal functionality, safety and comfort, regardless of their size.

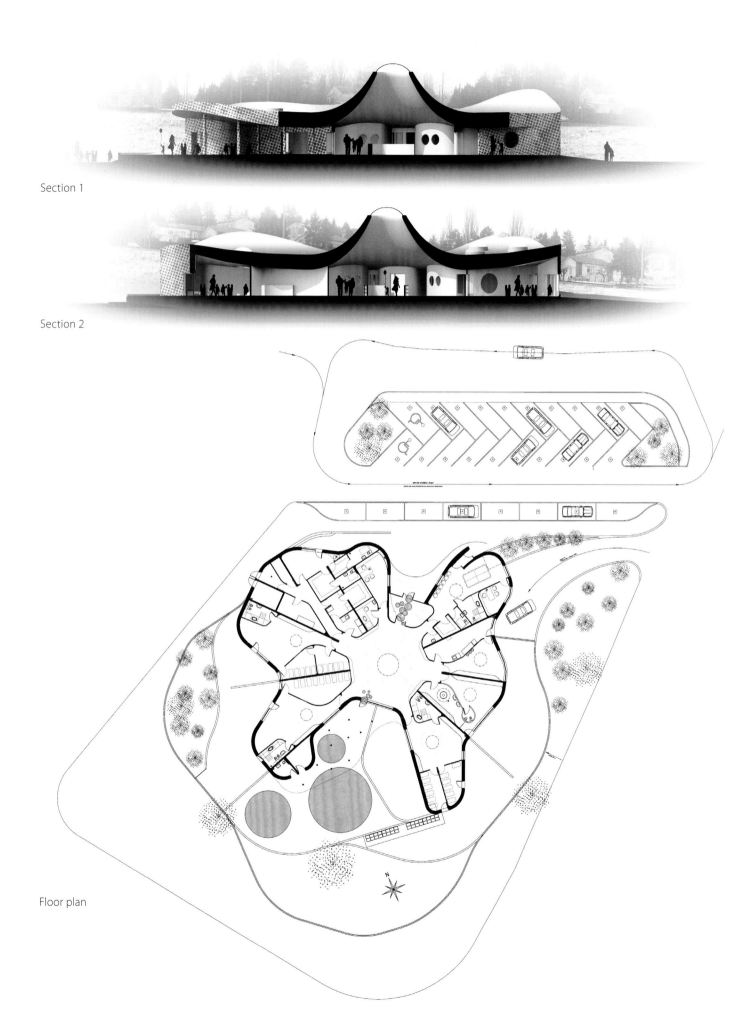

Section 1

Section 2

Floor plan

257

Section 3

Section 4

258

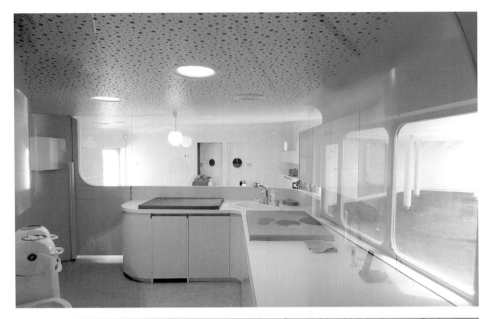

The interior of the building is organized around a highly protected circular central space. Children's spaces gravitate and converge around this center. Views between each part of the building are centrifugal and centripedal.

ZPZ Partners

Nido Caribimbi

Cavagnari, Parma, Italy

Photographs: contributed by ZPZ Partners

The project for this Nido (crèche or daycare) is based on two guidelines: a dialogue between pedagogy and architecture; and sustainability and focus on ecology. It is a company and municipal nursery for 48 children aged 12-36 months old, divided into two classes according to age. Ten places are available to children on municipal waiting lists, making it a public-private hybrid.

Nido Caribimbi aims to be a laboratory for children's self-learning, stimulating and supporting various journeys of development. The challenge for the architects was to build an environment for children in which the functional and aesthetic identity tells of and supports a precise image of the child: competent, an explorer, equipped with a hundred languages and great abilities. At the same time the project was conceived to use renewable energy sources (solar energy from photovoltaic solar panels), contain energy dispersal through a high level of insulation and thermal inertia, and use passive systems (the orientation of the building and covered porch areas) to provide protection from the sun's radiation.

The premises are organized in medium-sized areas, covered by a single roof and connected to each other by a central square which forms the hub of the nursery and is naturally illuminated by a large, round skylight. The classrooms and the "laboratories" (dining and atelier areas) are distributed towards the south to prioritize natural light and views of the setting; offices and service areas (laundry, changing rooms and store-room) are on the northern side and look onto the road. Classrooms are sub-divided into zones intended for diverse activities, and include a sleeping area, cloakroom spaces and bathrooms. This arrangement creates many spatial opportunities for activities while the sense of space remains on a scale suitable for the age-range of the children who attend the nursery.

The external cladding is vertical strips of wood in three colors and sizes. Arranged in a casual order, they continue into the sloping area under the outcrop of the roof, forming a pattern of varied grain which abuts softly into the green surroundings. The covered porch and the loggia of each wing appear as if hollowed from the mass of the building and are clad in vertical planks of coral-red wood. The imagery refers to the idea of a sliced fruit, where the flesh appears colored inside the textured exterior skin.

The project for the furnishings and interior details takes its starting point from the premise that environment – including architecture, furnishings, acoustics, color, light and the material landscape – is of fundamental importance in determining the pedagogical project, both in its capacity for influencing children in sensory and cognitive ways, and because the sensory qualities of an environment have strong empathy with the synaesthesia in the way a child learns. The environment must be flexible and fluctuating, as well as stimulating; this does not mean chaotic, confused, over-filled and noisy, but rather complex, variegated and rich in different languages and sensory stimuli.

Architecture:
ZPZ Partners
Architecture, interior design and construction administration:
Michele Zini, Claudia Zoboli,
Sara Michelini, Sara Callioni,
Maurizio Froghieri
Pedagogical consultancy:
Elisa Bulgheroni
Furniture:
PLAY+, Reggio Emilia
Client:
CariparmaCréditAgricole
Built area:
3,530 sqm (37,997 sqft)
Building area:
867 sqm (9,332 sqft)
Covered area:
1,189 sqm (12,798 sqft)

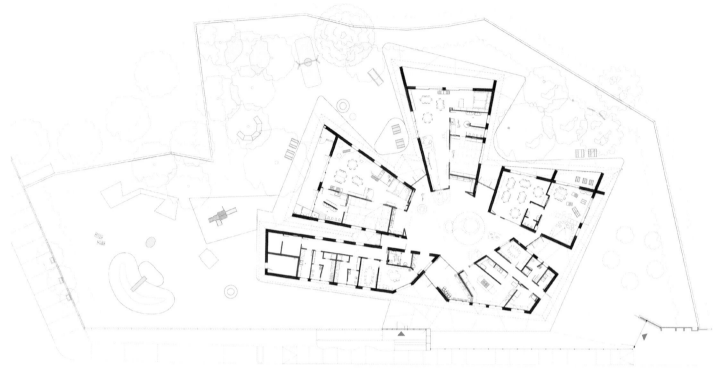

Site plan

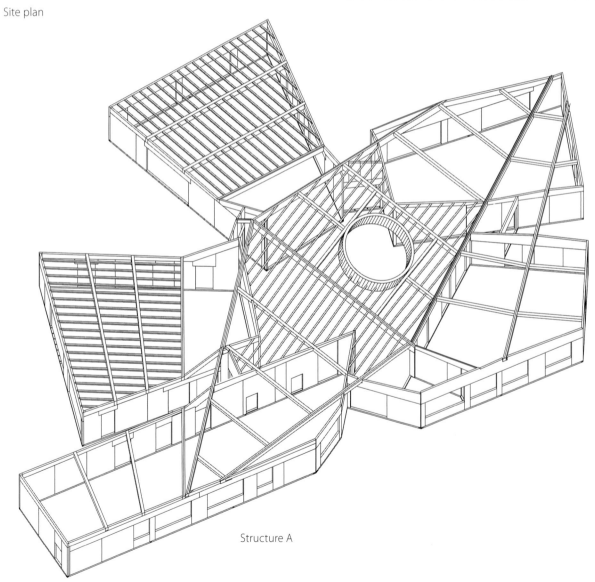

Structure A

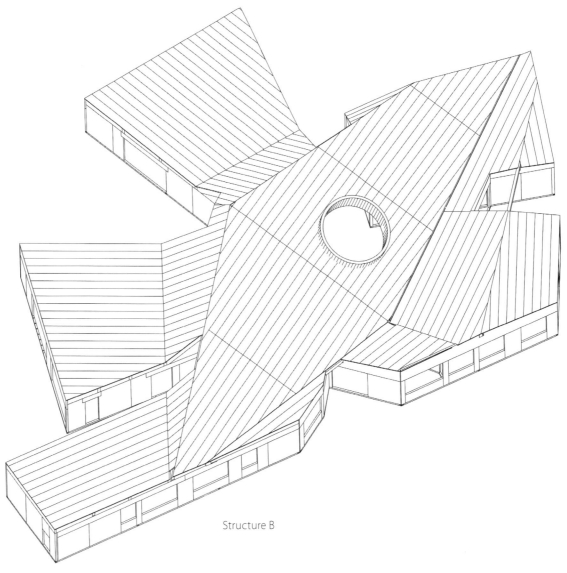

Structure B

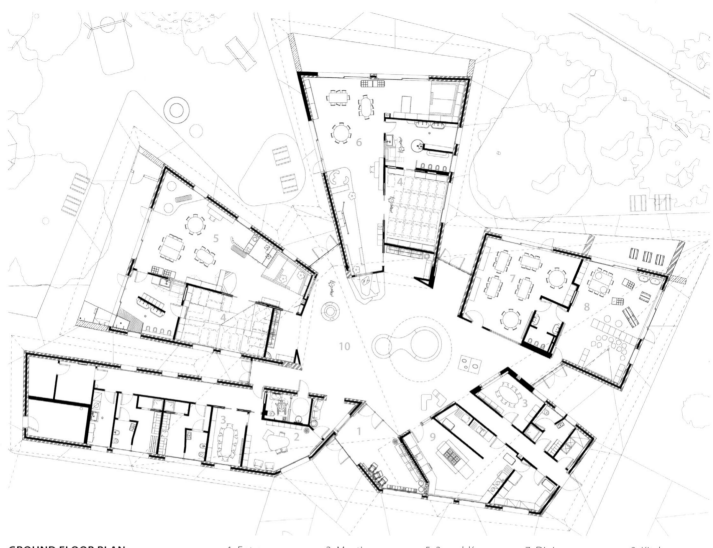

GROUND FLOOR PLAN

1. Entrance   3. Meeting room   5. 3 yr old´s room   7. Dining room   9. Kitchen

2. Office   4. Resting room   6. 1 yr old´s room   8. Ateller   10. Central piazza

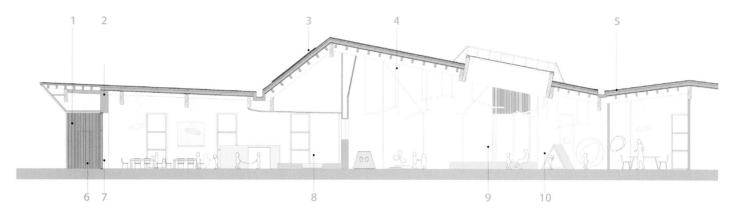

1. The exterior cladding is in vertical strips of wood in three colours and sizes, in a casual order. The covered porch and the loggia of each wing are clad in vertical planks of wood in a coral, red colour.
2. Wooden bearing structure (XLAM, 16,8cm thickness) and wood beams (20x70cm).
3. Rooftop photovoltaic vells (solar cells panels), south oriented, for generating electric power.
4. Suspended lighting fixtures, to create an intermediate ceiling in central square.
5. Roof sandwich, made of wooden structure, different layers of insulation, waterproofing membrane. total thermal transmittance U=1,18 W/m²K.
6. Each space has a dedicated loggia outdoor.
7. Vertical sandwich wall made of wooden structure, internal insulated gyspum board wall, external insulation and cladding. Total thermal transmittance U=1,13 W/m²k)
8. Classroom in pavilions
9. Gyspum board gate as entrance to classrooms: it handles changes of scale between piazza and pavilions and the hiding of air conditioning devices.
10. Central piazza where children of different ages meet; also for events, parents activities, small group activity.

The classrooms and the "laboratories" (dining and atelier areas) are distributed towards the south to prioritize natural light and views of the setting; offices and service areas (laundry, changing rooms and store-room) are on the northern side and look onto the road.

The design of the exterior of the building refers to the idea of a sliced fruit, where the flesh appears colored inside the textured exterior skin.

Bernardo Bader

Kindergarten Bizau

Bizau, Austria

Photographs: contributed by Bernardo Bader

The setting for this project in Bizau, Austria is marked by impressive views of the mountainous region of the Bregenz forest. The kindergarten has been designed to integrate into the built environment but at the same time create a connection with its natural surroundings.

The aim of the project was to provide a versatile, distinctive world for the children who use this facility. The premises comprise two classrooms, a playroom and a gym, with all the spaces marked by an aura of relaxation and "homely" architecture.

The façades of the timber structure are clad in silver fir, with generously proportioned windows that let in light and frame the spectacular landscape. The spacious interior structure is built entirely of local fir and ash, and the fittings were created by local carpenters who made use of the functional benefits of the wood. The quality of the timber is augmented by criteria like pollutant-free indoor air and an exceptional life cycle assessment. The building marks an intelligent contribution to the concepts of regionality, environmental compatibility and ecology.

Architecture:
Bernardo Bader
Area:
750 sqm (8,100 sqft)

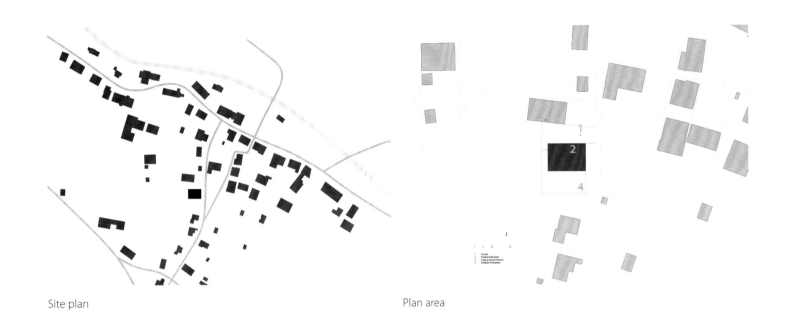

Site plan   Plan area

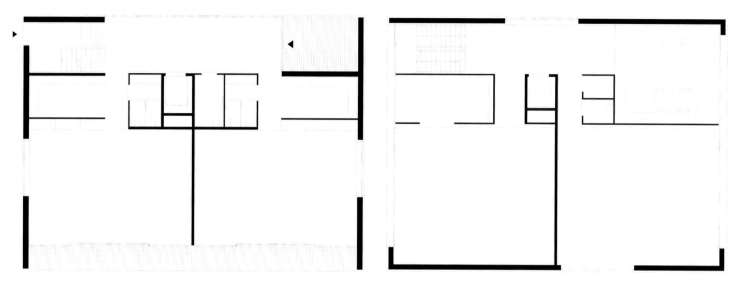

Plan ground floor   Plan upper floor

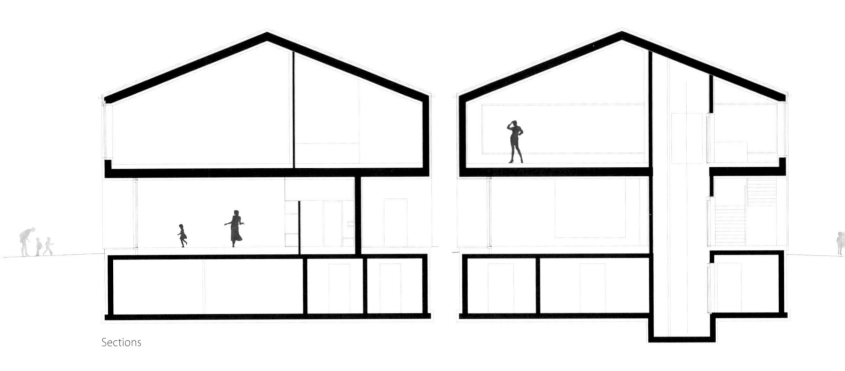

Sections

The facades of the timber structure are clad in silver fir, with generously proportioned windows that let in light and frame the spectacular landscape.

mipmarí arquitectura i disseny

Public Nursery in Ibiza

Ibiza, Spain

Photographs: Lourdes Grivé

This public nursery for children aged 0-3, in Can Coix in the municipality of Sant Antoni in Ibiza, is located on a rustic plot of land adjoining an already-existing school and municipal center. The land is typically Mediterranean in terms of vegetation, with pines, holm oaks and shrub bushes, and the nursery aims to integrate naturally into this setting.

The program occupies only one floor, and is built in fractured volumes so as to preserve the protected trees and Mediterranean atmosphere, and to create a pleasant transition between interior and exterior space, with natural illumination and ventilation and a play of light and shadows under the pines.An entrance courtyard provides access from the street.

Inside, the design of the hallways and transitional spaces seeks to recreate the atmosphere typical to Mediterranean streets, which are places of meeting, interaction, and children´s play. The space is bright, minimizing the difference between outside and in, creating potential for education to continue fluidly outside the center in the form of group activities.

The five classrooms are located along the south-east façade, grouped by age. Services have been placed on the northern side of the building, to help filter out the noise pollution from the street.

The distribution of the building aims to be climatically passive, with the roof serving as another façade. With an end to simplifying the construction and maintanence, and at the same time creating visual uniformity, the minimum possible number of materials were used. After considering various proposed materials, mortar was chosen, and its unified application creates continuity between roofs and façades, interiors and exteriors, and creates a visual impact as the white walls wind and cross through the plot, defining and demarcating space for access and play.

The building, dazzling white against the green and brown hilly landscape, is modern in appearance and yet in complete harmony with the cultural and architectural heritage it is derived from.

Architecture:
mipmarí arquitectura i disseny
(Txell Manresa, Toni Marí and David Pareras)
Engineer:
Antonio Roig Marí
Collaborators:
Noèlia Asensi, Erik Herrera, Alicia Torres,
Jesús Rodríguez, Daniel Roig, Carlos Juan,
Xavier Aguado (structure),
Mif (measurements)
Client:
Consell Insular d'Eivissa
Construction:
Estel ingeniería y obras
Area:
600 sqm (6,500 sqft)

The program occupies only one floor, and is built in fractured volumes so as to preserve the protected trees and to create a pleasant transition between interior and exterior space.

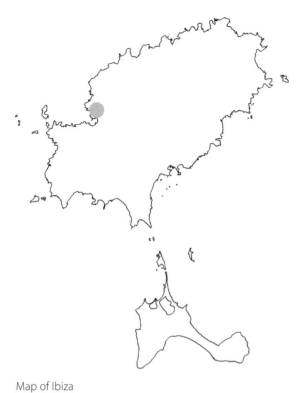

Map of Ibiza

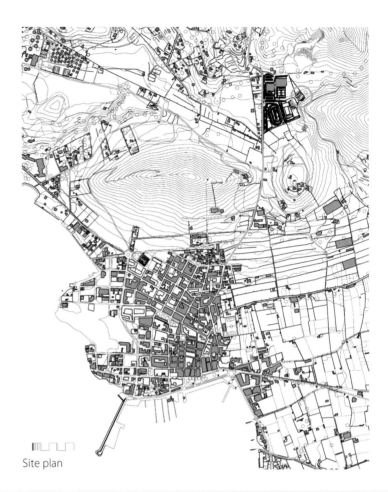

Site plan

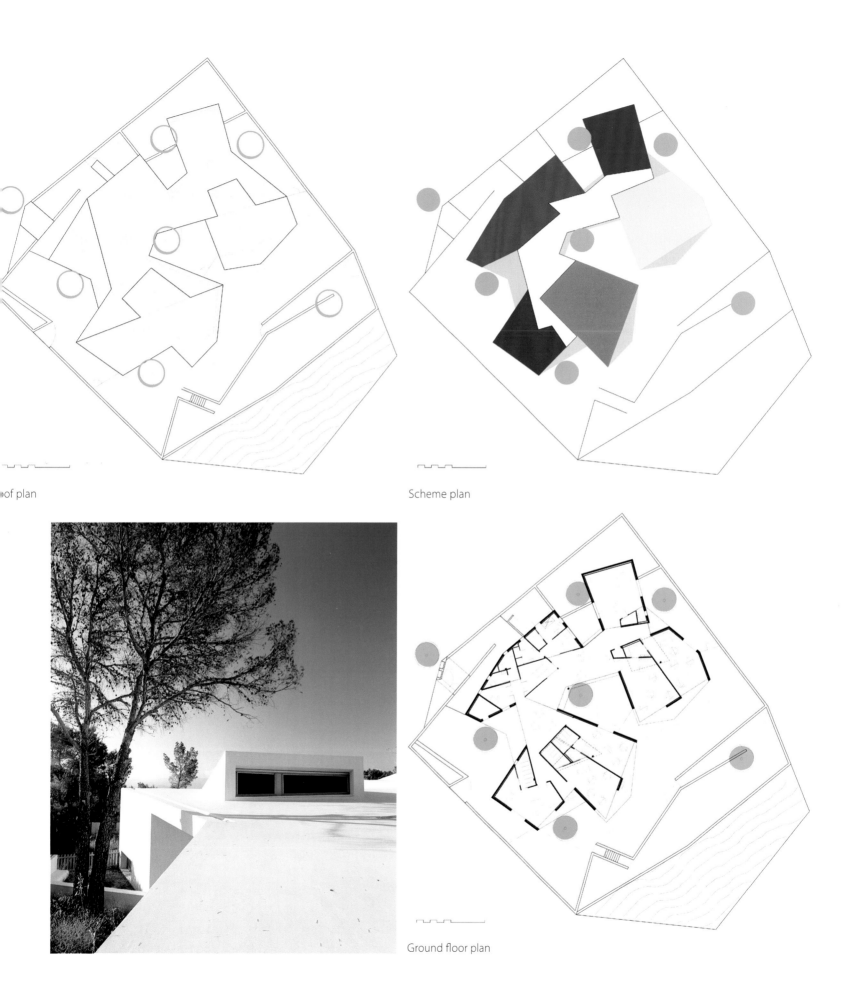

of plan

Scheme plan

Ground floor plan

Elevations

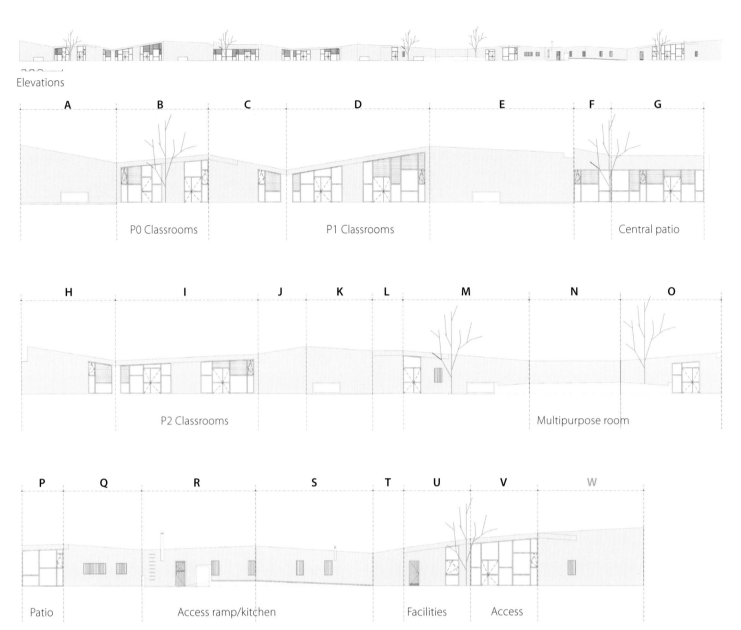

A   B   C   D   E   F   G

P0 Classrooms   P1 Classrooms   Central patio

H   I   J   K   L   M   N   O

P2 Classrooms   Multipurpose room

P   Q   R   S   T   U   V   W

Patio   Access ramp/kitchen   Facilities   Access

Inside, the design of the hallways and transitional spaces seeks to recreate the atmosphere typical to Mediterranean streets, which are places of meeting, interaction, and children´s play.

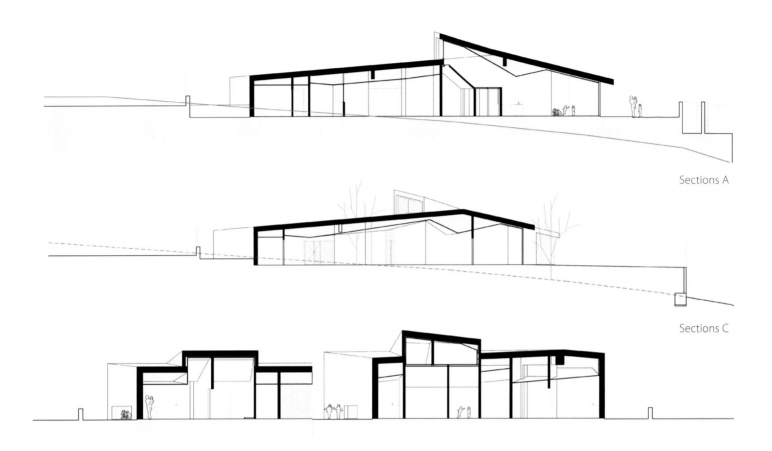

Sections A

Sections C

Sections D

After considering various proposed materials, mortar was chosen, and its unified application creates continuity between roofs and façades, interiors and exteriors, and creates a visual impact as the white walls wind and cross through the plot, defining and demarcating space for access and play.

With an end to simplifying the construction and maintanence, and at the same time create visual uniformity, the minimum possible number of materials were used.

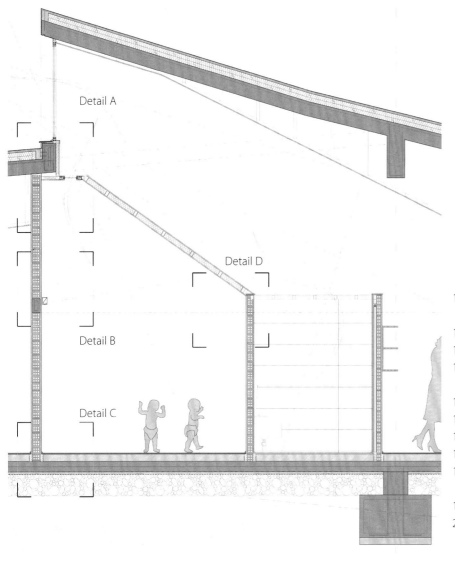

1. Rockwool insulation
2. Gypsum plasterboards, 15mm thick
3. Gypsum plasterboards, 15mm thick
4. Ceramic brick, 9x12x24cm
5. Ceramic tiles, 30x60cm
6. Plaster painted with outdoor plastic paint
7. Ceramic brick 9x12x24 cm
8. Plaster painted with outdoor plastic paint
9. DM skirting waterproof coating
10. Self-leveling mortar layer, between 4 and 6mm
11. Linoleum flooring, 3,5mm thick
12. Reinforced concrete floor, 15cm
13. Extruded polyester insulation, 5cm
14. Plastic separating sheet
15. Crushed limestone base, 20cm
16. Geotextile sheet
17. Layer of leveling mortar
18. Galvanized steel tubular subframe 2 = 2mm
19. Aluminum dropper
20. Polymer concrete crowning
21. Cork perimeter joints
22. Aluminum cap, 2mm
23. Gypsum plasterboards, 15mm
24. Rockwool insulation
25. Galvanized steel substructure for fixing plasterboard
26. Galvanized steel substructure for fixing plasterboard
27. Gypsum plasterboards, 15mm
28. Swinging window cover
29. Window substructure

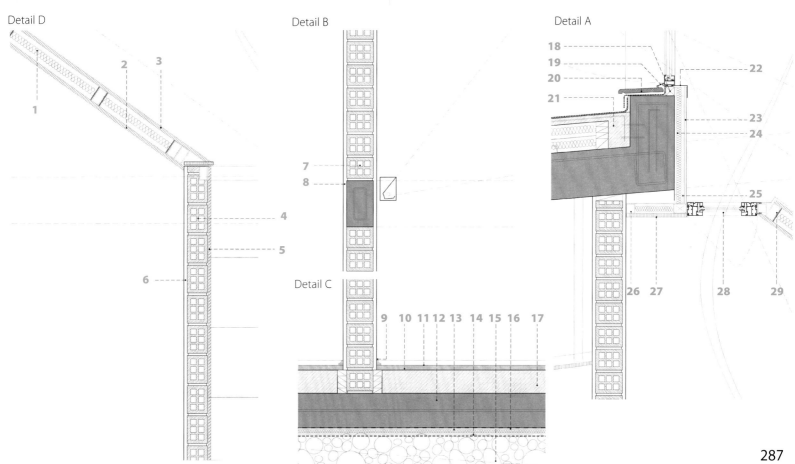

287

AIR / Cyrille Hanappe & Olivier Leclercq

Children's Recreation Center

Pierrelaye, France

Photographs: David Boureau

The Children's Recreation Center is located in Pierrelaye, a small rural town in France, and is surrounded by agricultural warehouses. The plan for the project took into account the particular layout of the lot, and the building is accessed by a narrow path stretching into the site.

The main structure follows and reinforces the urban pattern, becoming an articulation and a filter between the town and this domain reserved for children. Seen from the street the single volume structure, covered entirely with mechanical tiles, blends in with other buildings in the area. However, on the other side the premises reveal small, colored houses in varying shapes and sizes which open onto a garden designed specifically for young people.

The Children's Recreation Center is characterized by bright and cheerful colors. Structural elements inside the buildings are also designed in primary hues, creating an inviting environment. This is reinforced by the light, airy atmosphere of the interior, the result of floor to ceiling glazing which forms a connection with the exterior.

Architecture:
AIR / CyrilleHanappe &
Olivier Leclercq
Architects in charge:
Estelle Nicod, William Loupias
Client:
City of Pierrelaye
Site area:
5,250 sqm (56,511 sqft)
Constructed area:
1,500 sqm (16,400 sqft)

Seen from the street the single volume structure, covered entirely with mechanical tiles, blends in with other buildings in the area.

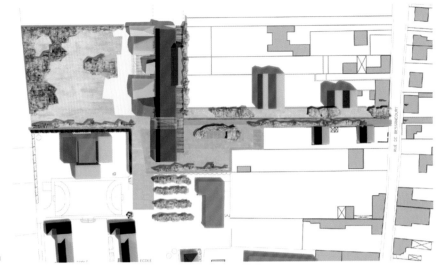

Site plan

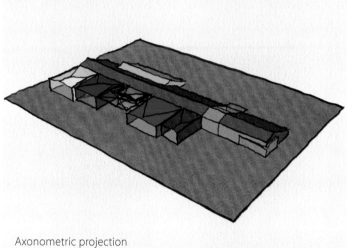

Axonometric projection

GROUND FLOOR PLAN

1. Covered entrance	11. Office	21. Kitchen workshop
2. Lobby	12. Meeting room	22. Nature workshop
3. Reception	13. Washrooms	23. Covered patio
4. Playroom	14. Dindos Room	24. Castros Room
5. Animation room	15. Blg Boss Room	25. Bisounoups Room
6. Men´s changeroom	16. Malabars Room	26. Workshop
7. Changeroom, Wm	17. Pichous Room	27. Lutins Room
8. Boiler	18. Laundry	28. Sleeping room
9. Technical room	19. Space	
10. Office	20. Multiuse room	

Structural elements inside the buildings are also designed in primary colors, creating an inviting environment.

Longitudinal elevation

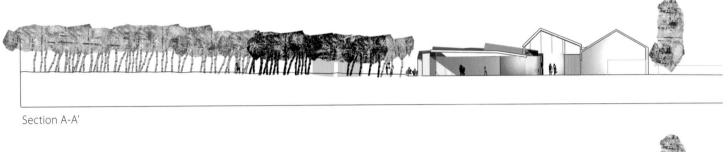

Section A-A'

Section B-B'

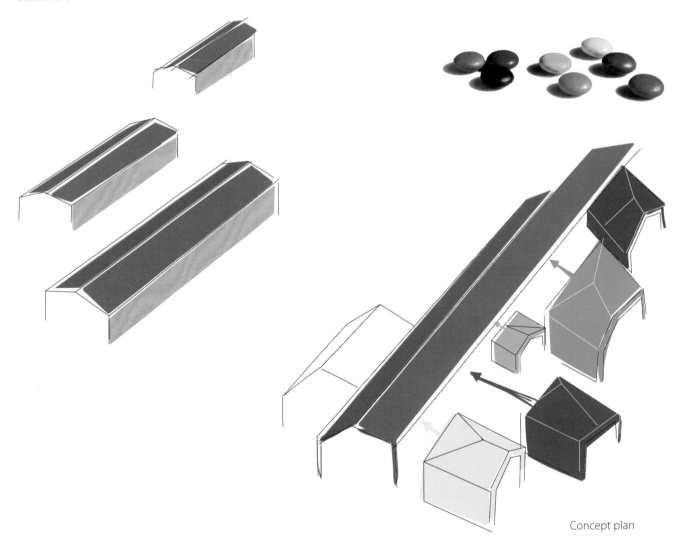

Concept plan

Xavier Vilalta

Arreletes Day Care Center

Els Alamús, Lleida, Spain

Photographs: Jordi Anguera

Els Alamús is a small village with seven hundred inhabitants, situated on a hill in the middle of the Lleida plain. The surrounding area is predominantly agricultural fields and fruit trees – a planned and designed geometric landscape which is the result of man's work and engineering.

The nursery is located on the edge of the urbanization, next to the only road into the village. It is surrounded by a sports area, an orchard that will be transformed into a plaza in the future and a slope that separates the level of the houses and the countryside.

The project created two volumes: the lower one, supported by an existing agricultural wall and following the direction of the fields, houses the classrooms and the courtyard; the second space – which follows the direction of the houses in the village – overlooks the children's courtyard and accommodates the teachers' offices. Both spaces provide access to the building and are connected by a staircase inserted into the natural slope.

Personal memories of a childhood spent in shade-filtered spaces among countless, perfectly organized fruit treescontributed to the design of the classrooms. The areas are versatile, continuous and have controlled lighting. The foyer and the first classroom can be transformed into a dining hall and the classrooms – which are connected to the courtyard through the changing rooms – are orientated to the east through a large horizontal window that rests on the slope. A pixilated image of leaves gives the interior corridor screened light from the west, and colored glass in the passageways creates a fun atmosphere for the children.

Industrial materials including steel, concrete, glass and wood were used for the construction, and a roof garden was incorporated into the design.

Architecture:
Xavier Vilalta
Architect team:
Xavier Vilalta, Margarita Félix, Sonia Maia
Project manager:
Mario Campos
Structure:
GN Arquitectos
Contractor:
Hnos Ojeda
Client:
Alamús Council
Area:
254 sqm (2,734 sqft)

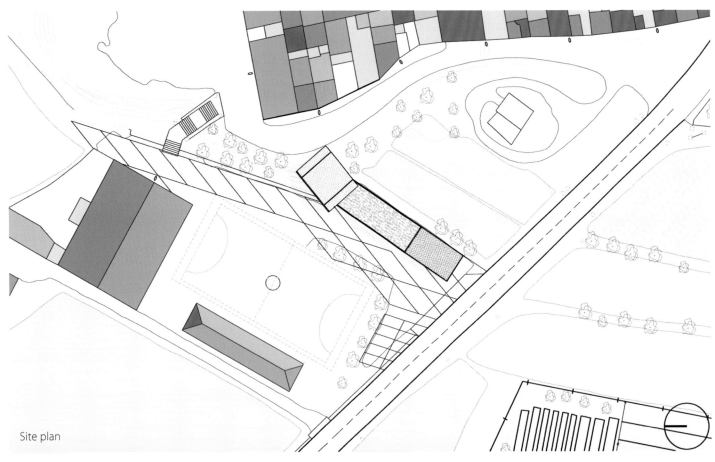

Site plan

First floor plan

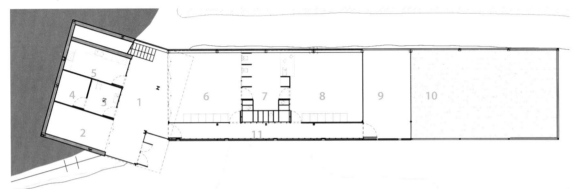

Ground floor plan

1. Hall
2. Trolley storage
3. WC
4. Facilities
5. Kitchen
6. Classroom 1
7. Bathroom
8. Classroom 2
9. Porch
10. Terrace 1
11. Corridor
12. Teacher's room
13. Administration
14. Staircase

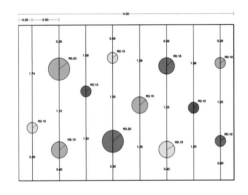

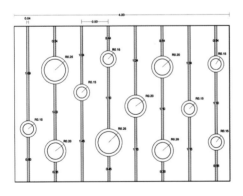

Details and section

Wall geometry

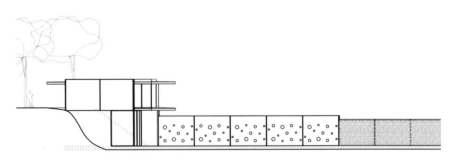

Section A-A'

Facade 1

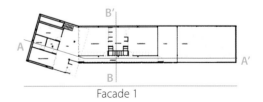

Facade 1

Section BB'

Axonometry of façade and roof

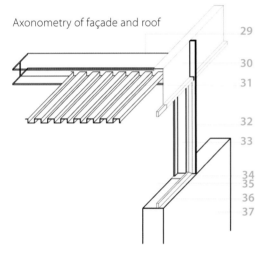

29
30
31
32
33
34
35
36
37

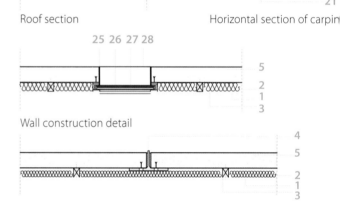

Construction detail of roof and façade

Roof section

Horizontal section of carpin

Wall construction detail

KEY

1. Table DM 1cm coated with plastic paint
2. High density polyurethane thermal insulation, 40mm
3. Wooden rod forming the structure of the wooden wall
4. Profile HEB 260
5. Prefabricated concrete panel 100mm
   Formatin ecologial roof
6. Strainless steel coating (5mm) dark grey
7. Insulation FELTEMPER 300P
8. Flagstone FILTRON
9. Selected plants
10. Planted substrate
11. High density plyurethane thermal insulation, 40mm
12. Water proofing membrane, moisture barrier 80mm
13. Leveling floor
14. Concrete for a composite slab
15. Mesh cast 5mm slab decking 150x150mm
16. Corrugated iron 5mmx60mm
17. Profile HEB 220
18. Suspended ceiling of plasterboard with aluminum frame
19. Profile IPN 200

20. Perforated brick
21. Metal plate e=80mm
22. Stainless steel dark grey counterframe for the window
23. Aluminum frame
24. Safety glass 4+4/6/4+4mm
25. Metal counterframe for forming the hole of the window
26. Glass 10mm
27. Supply and fix aluminium sheet metal roof ridge, 400mm
28. Vinyl board of different colors according to sizes
29. Profile HEB 200
30. Stainless steel coating e=50mm h 530xL3920mm
31. Corrugated iron 5mmx60mm
32. Metal plate e=80mm
33. Profile IPN 200
34. Platten stainless steel for pillar support
35. Glass
36. Metalwork
37. Prefabricated concrete panel

A pixilated image of leaves gives the interior corridor screened light from the west, and colored glass in the passageways creates a fun atmosphere for the children. The classrooms are orientated to the east through a large horizontal window that rests on the slope.

aap.architekten

Askew in the vaults - Kindergarten at Schönbrunn Palace

Vienna, Austria

Photographs: Rupert Steiner

Wiener Kinderfreunde have been running a kindergarten at Schönbrunn Palace, one of Austria's cultural assets, since the 1950s. However, it no longer met the spatial requirements of today's kindergartens so the former imperial kitchen that had served for decades as a storage area was converted to accommodate four groups of children.

The empty space seemed dauntingly high and had very poor acoustics. The window sills were 1.75 m (5 ft 9 in) above the floor, so even the adults could not see outside. To break through the austerity of these historical spaces with their strikingly high Bohemian vaults, a large structure, like an oversized piece of furniture, was placed with its main axis slightly askew to the orthogonal grid. The break was further reinforced by the additional nesting of spaces on the newly created second level. Most of the built-in wooden elements are lower than room height and the gaps between them and the vaults were closed off with glass or stainless steel mesh. The effect is finished by panels of light-colored Finnish birch covering the walls and children's furniture throughout the space.

The high casement windows are protected historical features of the building, so children's windows were installed beneath them, along the base of the wall. From outside they are seen as plain glass panels, but inside they are niches with a lookout, which are popular with the children and also serve to let more natural light into the building.

The adverse acoustic conditions were addressed by a building physicist who installed appropriate sound-absorbing surfaces and bolted quadratic acousticpanels to the ceiling. The measurements conducted once this had been done revealed good acoustic values, subjectively and objectively. The old floor had no insulation whatsoever, so it was replaced with a floor slab featuring appropriate thermal insulation and topped by a new heatable floor. Wherever official regulations allowed ecological materials were used, including wood paneling, linoleum or wooden floors and wooden constructions made from panels of Finnish birch to separate the rooms.

The differing levels, niches, vistas and outlooks mean that none of the spaces are the same and there is always something new to discover, and the cozy "living room" atmosphere is in conscious contrast to the stringent baroque environment. The children and educators were integrated in the planning process of the project, and so were able to familiarize themselves gradually with their new environment.

This contemporary kindergarten project was successfully integrated into a building which is protected as an historical monument. It will continue to meet functional and educational requirement for decades to come.

Architecture:
aap.architekten
Project team:
Roswitha Siegl, Marie Pertlwieser,
Hans Früh, Franz Ryznar
Construction:
Prof.DI Hans Baumgartner
Building physics:
Mag.Wolfgang Hebenstreit
Carpentry:
Zimmerei Fuss
Clients:
Die Kinderfreunde,
Schloß Schönbrunn Kultur-
und Betriebsges.m.b.H.
Area:
365 sqm (3,900 sqft)

Ground floor plan

0   1   5

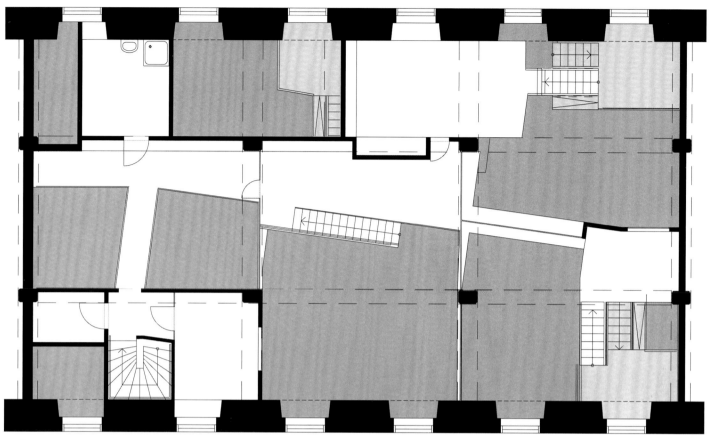

1st floor plan

To break through the austerity of the historical spaces with their strikingly high Bohemian vaults, a large structure, like an oversized piece of furniture, was placed with its main axis slightly askew to the orthogonal grid.

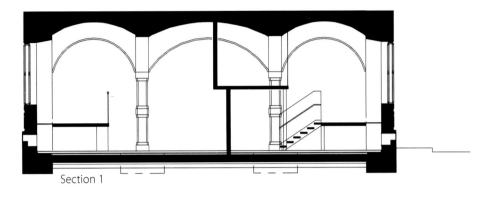

Section 1

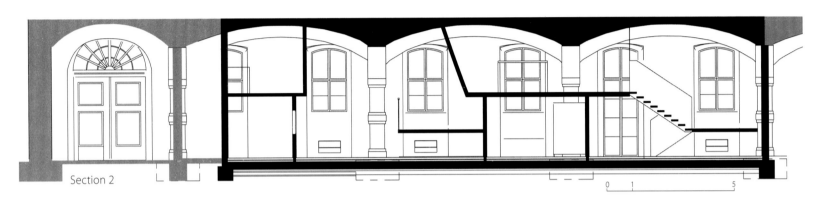

Section 2

0 1   5

Wherever official regulations allowed ecological materials were used, including wood paneling, linoleum or wooden floors and wooden constructions made from panels of Finnish birch to separate the rooms.

Elisa Valero Ramos

Day care in El Serrallo

Granada, Spain

Photographs: Fernando Alda

Serrallo is located in the north of Granada and marks the division between the city and the foothills of the Sierra Nevada. The day care is intended for children of up to 3 years of age and the design consists of 7 units, with a total capacity for 102 children.

Due to the pleasant climate of the region, the program includes direct access from the play zone to the slope of the mountain behind, so as to encourage, even at this young age, contact with nature.

The marked topography of the plot and the wish to orient the building so that the classrooms have appealing views was a key determinant in the many of the planning decisions. Due to uneven terrain, the building was constructed on two levels with direct access between them. The materials were chosen according to their rational use, and economical and construction considerations. The exterior has been finished in materials that don't require maintenance, such as concrete, which envelops the building along vertical and horizontal parameters like a shell, and the glazed ceramics enclosures used on the east and west sides.

The playful nature of the recreational area has been reinforced by geometric wall murals in vibrant colors, designed by the artist Eduardo Barco. The interior of the building, in contrast, makes use of neutral materials, predominantly white and tile.

Due to seismic activity in Granada and the low resistance of the land reported by the geotechnical study, a 7 meter (22 ft) retaining wall of reinforced concrete has been integrated into the design to support the difference in height between the two sides of the project.

The building has been constructed to be bioclimatic. It takes advantage of the energy gained through sunlight in the classrooms and passageways in winter, and controls the entrance of light in the summer, reducing the need for external conditioning systems.

The materials used throughout are in keeping with traditional materials from the region: glazed ceramics produced in the same way as those that in the 12th century were made to cover the Alhambra. In particular, the lattice of the west façade is a contemporary reference to traditional Arab latticework. The interior space is defined by white and light spaces, a constant in Mediterranean architecture through the ages.

Architecture:
Elisa Valero Ramos

Quantity surveyor:
María de los Llanos Martín Romero

Collaborators:
Leonardo Tapiz Buzarra, architect;
Esteban Salcedo and Óscar Raya,
architecture students

Client:
Department of Urbanism, Ayuntamiento de
Granada

Construction:
Aldesa Construcciones S.A.

Built area:
900 sqm (9,700 sqft)

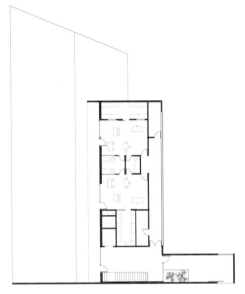

First floor plan

Due to the pleasant climate of the region, the program includes direct access from the play zone to the slope of the mountain behind, so as to encourage, even at this young age, contact with nature.

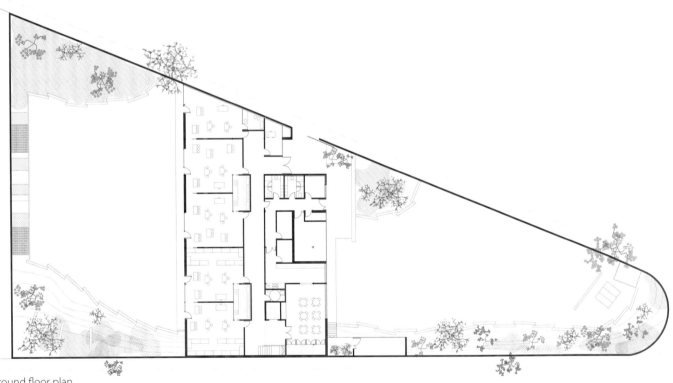

Ground floor plan

The exterior has been finished in materials that don't require maintenance, such as concrete, which envelops the building along vertical and horizontal parameters like a shell, and the glazed ceramics enclosures used on the east and west sides.

Section

The materials used throughout are in keeping with traditional materials from the region: glazed ceramics produced in the same way as those that in the 12th century were made to cover the Alhambra. In particular, the lattice of the west façade is a contemporary reference to traditional Arab latticework. The interior space is defined by white and light spaces, a constant in Mediterranean architecture through the ages.